*T*his book
belongs to

Sheila Murray

...a woman after God's
own heart.

9104420

Cultivating a Life of Character

Elizabeth George

HARVEST HOUSE PUBLISHERS
Eugene, Oregon 97402

Cover by Terry Dugan Design, Minneapolis, Minnesota

Acknowledgments

As always, thank you to my dear husband, Jim George, M.Div., Th.M., for your able assistance, guidance, suggestions, and loving encouragement on this project

Contents

Foreword

For some time I have been looking for Bible studies that I could use each day that would increase my knowledge of God's Word. In my search, I found myself struggling between two extremes: Bible studies that required little time but also had little substance, or studies that were in-depth and demanded more time than I could give. I discovered that I wasn't alone—there were many other women like me who were busy yet desired to spend quality time studying God's Word.

That's why I became excited when Elizabeth George shared her desire to create a series of women's Bible studies that offered in-depth lessons that could be completed in just 15-20 minutes per day. When she completed the first study—on Philippians—I was eager to try it out. I had already studied Philippians many times, but this was the first time I had come to understand exactly how the whole book fit together and how it can truly be lived out in my life. Each lesson was simple but insightful—and was written especially to apply to me as a woman!

In the Woman After God's Own Heart® Bible study series, Elizabeth takes you step by step through the Scriptures, sharing wisdom she has gleaned from more than 20 years as a women's Bible teacher. The lessons are rich and meaningful because they're rooted in God's Word and have been lived out in Elizabeth's life. Her thoughtful and personable guidance make you feel as though you are studying right alongside her—as if she is personally mentoring you in the greatest aspiration you could ever pursue: to become a woman after God's own heart.

If you're looking for Bible studies that can help you grow stronger in your knowledge of God's Word even in the most demanding of schedules, I know you'll find this series to be a welcome companion in your daily walk with God.

—LaRae Weikert
Editorial Managing Director,
Harvest House Publishers

Before You Begin

*I*n my book *A Woman After God's Own Heart,®* I describe such a woman as one who ensures that God is first in her heart and the Ultimate Priority of her life. Then I share that one crucial way this desire can become reality is by nurturing a heart that abides in God's Word. To do so means that you and I must develop a root system anchored deep in God's Word.

Before you launch into this Bible study, take a moment to think about these aspects of a root system produced by the regular, faithful study of God's Word:

- *Roots are unseen*—You'll want to set aside time in solitude—"underground" if you will—to immerse yourself in God's Word and grow in Him.

- *Roots are for taking in*—Alone and with your Bible in hand, you'll want to take in and feed upon the truths of the Word of God and ensure your spiritual growth.

- *Roots are for storage*—As you form the habit of looking into God's Word, you'll find a vast, deep reservoir of divine hope and strength forming for the rough times.

- *Roots are for support*—Do you want to stand strong in the Lord? To stand firm against the pressures of life? The routine care of your roots through exposure to God's Word will cultivate you into a remarkable woman of endurance.[1]

I'm glad you've chosen this study out of my A Woman After God's Own Heart® Bible study series. My prayer for you is that the truths you find in God's Word through this study will further transform your life into the image of His dear Son and empower you to be the woman you seek to be: a woman after God's own heart.

In His love,

Elizabeth George

Serving the Lord

Introduction

"It was the best of times, it was the worst of times." So begins Charles Dickens' classic book *A Tale of Two Cities*.

Well, my friend, we could well use these same words to describe the times during the period of the books of Judges and Ruth, which we are about to study together! Why? Because the "best of times" and "the worst of times" accurately report Israel's situation throughout these two God-inspired books of the Bible.

But before we inspect the portraits of the men and women who fill the pages of these two historical books of the Old Testament, and before we make our way through the good, the bad, and the ugly details of both Judges and Ruth, here are a few gems you can look forward to discovering along the way:

The constant faithfulness of God
The forgiveness and grace of God
The power and repeated deliverance of God
The redeeming work of God
The raising up of a variety of unlikely heroes by God

Now, dear one, let's discover God's message to our heart.

God's Message...

To better understand the situation of God's people, let's begin with a look at the life of God's warrior Joshua, a man who most definitely lived a life of character!

1. After God appointed Joshua to succeed Moses as the leader of God's people, what did God say to him concerning the land (Joshua 1:6)?

   Now look at the map on page 141 and inspect the extent of God's provision for the children of Israel.

2. What was God's desire for Joshua with regard to the law of Moses (Joshua 1:8)?

3. And what was God's assurance to Joshua (Joshua 1:9)?

   At the end of his life, Joshua gathered the people together for a review of God's faithfulness (Joshua 24:1-13). As one scholar-of-old noted about these scriptures, "Joshua had witnessed God's faithfulness for 40 years in the brick kilns, 40 years in the desert, and 30 years in the promised land, and this was his dying testimony."[2]

Quickly note...Joshua's final challenge to the people (Joshua 24:14-15)—

...the people's response and why (Joshua 24:16-18)—

...Joshua's warning...and the people's response (Joshua 24:20-21)—

Well, my friend, the stage is now set for the books of Judges and Ruth—

- ✓ Joshua had performed the role of an outstanding spiritual leader.
- ✓ The conquest of the land had begun.
- ✓ The people were challenged to follow the Lord.
- ✓ Joshua would soon die.
- ✓ The people must now fulfill God's commands to them to finish conquering the land and to set up a nation that would serve God with their whole heart.

The next 24 lessons will be exciting ones, I can assure you, as you and I witness together the triumphs and failures of God's people in serving the Lord and carrying out their mission.

...and Your Heart's Response

You'll discover as we make our way through this Bible study that your heart's response is vital. Why? Because one purpose of all Bible study is to change your life. As women after God's own heart, we want our hearts and lives to resemble more and more the heart and life of Jesus Christ.

So let's see what changes we can—or must!—make and what character qualities we can—or must!—better cultivate.

God's servant Joshua sets such a fine example for us as a person of great character for many reasons:

- Joshua was a *student of God's Word*. What does 2 Timothy 3:15-16 teach us about the necessity and practice of being a student of God's Word?

  And Acts 17:11?

  And 1 Peter 2:1-2?

  How do you think being a student of God's Word relates to cultivating a life of character?

- Joshua was *strong in the Lord*. What commands and promises are given to you and me for finding our strength in the Lord in...

  ...Ephesians 6:10—

  ...Philippians 4:13—

  ...2 Timothy 1:7—

  Where do you generally look for strength, and how can you remember to look upward—to the Lord—for His much-needed strength?

- Joshua was *submissive to God's commands*. Love for God is key when it comes to being submissive to God's commands. What does John 14:15 have to say about our love and our obedience to God?

And 1 John 5:2-3?

And Luke 6:46?

*F*ailure to keep the law is always the outcome of failure in love to the Lawgiver.[3]

How's your love for the Lawgiver? Can you look beyond the commands of Scripture to the One who is sending forth the command? How does Colossians 3:23 help as you develop a heart of obedience?

- Joshua *served God wholeheartedly*. Numerous times Joshua challenged the Israelites to serve God whole-heartedly (Joshua 24:14-23). Why so repeatedly? Possibly (and probably!) because Joshua knew from firsthand devotion and experience what serving God wholeheart-edly entailed. After all, he had faithfully served God— and found God faithful—for 110 years! What prayer did David pray in Psalm 86:11, and how do you think praying (and meaning!) such a heartfelt prayer yourself would help you in your quest for the character quality of whole-hearted service to God?

- Joshua *showed others an example of character*. We need models of the Christian faith. What does Titus 2:3-5 say about modeling and mentoring?

• Who is your model? And what are you doing to develop your character so that you can (by God's grace!) model for others what it means to serve the Lord?

Cultivating a Life of Character

How easy it is to glibly gush (as did the Israelites), "Oh, of course, we will serve the Lord!" However, rash promises are sometimes hard to fulfill. Joshua, unlike the people he led, didn't make any rash commitments. Instead he cultivated a life of character by faithfully devoting himself to God, to serving Him, and doing so according to His Word.

What a blessing it is here in our first lesson to discover *the* first lesson about serving the Lord God! Here we've met a true man of character. We've looked at what it took for Joshua to be a man of character, a man in good standing with God. Perhaps the following words say it best to our hearts. Read them...and then make your own heart response: What must—and will!—*you* do about your own commitment to serve the Lord?

> The call to commitment is a call to constant vigilance in maintaining and understanding the standards of that commitment. No matter what distractions a godly leader may encounter, he or she needs to maintain his or her focus on serving the Lord.[4]

Following Through

Judges 1:1-36

*I'*ll never forget the once-in-a-lifetime camping trip Jim and I took to Yellowstone National Park in Wyoming. The season was early summer. And the flowers were just coming into full bloom. The first thing we did when we arrived in the Park was head straight to a crop of flat rocks where we stood with hundreds of other tourists to wait for the next scheduled (yes, scheduled!) eruption of the geyser known as "Old Faithful." Supposedly it got its name because a watch can actually be set by the geyser's eruptions!

Before we study who could and who couldn't be counted on by God after the death of Joshua, let's lay one more layer of foundation upon which to build our understanding of the books of Judges and Ruth by asking and answering a few questions.

Who wrote the books of Judges and Ruth? Probably the prophet Samuel. Jewish tradition credits Samuel as the author, as he lived at the time some of the events of these two books of the Bible took place (1 Samuel 10:25).

Where do the events of Judges and Ruth take place? "The Promised Land" is the setting for both Judges and Ruth, the land of Canaan, later called Israel. (See the map on page 141.)

When was this pair of books written? Judges was probably written around the beginning of King Saul's reign (about 1045 B.C.), and, based on the timing of David's anointing by Samuel, Ruth followed afterward.

Why were these two historical books written? Together, both books give an unvarnished description of the history of God's people over a period of roughly three centuries. Judges teaches us that turning away from Jehovah incurs severe punishment and that turning back to God restores joy and well-being. And Ruth, the beautiful little book of Ruth, points to our loving Lord's redeeming work in the lives of three people who remained strong in character and faithful to Him while the society around them was collapsing in moral decay.

God's Message...

1. Read now the first chapter of Judges. Check here when you are finished. _____

2. As we step into this lesson *and* the book of Judges, note the opening event (verse 1).

What two tribes of the Israelite people went up to fight against the Canaanites (verses 3-4)?

And, in a few words, what was the outcome (verses 4-5)?

3. As these conquering tribes moved south from the city of Jerusalem (verse 8) to the hill country (verse 10) (see your map on page 141), what challenge and promise did Caleb put forth (verse 12)?

Who followed through on Caleb's challenge, and what was his reward (verse 13)?

What bold—and wise!—request did Caleb's daughter Achsah make of her father (verse 15)?

4. What good report does God give about Caleb (verse 20)?

And "the house of Joseph," the combined tribes of Ephraim and Manasseh (verses 22-25)?

In contrast, what bad report does God give regarding the tribes of Israel in the following verses?

Judah (verse 19)—

Benjamin (verse 21)—

Manasseh (verse 27)—

Ephraim (verse 29)—

Zebulun (verse 30)—

Asher (verses 31-32)—

Naphtali (verse 33)—

Dan (verse 34)—

...and Your Heart's Response

As we, as women after God's own heart, seek to cultivate lives of faithful character, let's look to the "characters" from Judges for instruction on how to follow through for God.

- *The Israelite tribes*—In a few words, pinpoint the negative trait(s) that most accurately describes their character as a whole.

Beloved, we are looking failure...and the consequences of failure...right in the eye. What does Luke 16:10 say about faithfulness?

Are there any tasks—small or large—that you are failing to follow through on and complete for God? Are there any roles where you are failing to live up to God's commands and requirements? As an exercise in follow-through, make a "To Do" list right now that reflects active steps you can—and must!—take to complete God's assignment(s) to you. Write out your situation/challenge below. Then check here when your "To Do" list is made.

- *Caleb*—Caleb has been tagged as "the Israelites' *can-do* person" and as a man with a mission. We noted from Judges 1:20 that Caleb was one of the few Israelites who followed through to the full in taking their inheritance and driving out the Canaanites. In a few words, pinpoint the positive trait(s) that most accurately describes Caleb's character.

What does Philippians 3:13-14 advise regarding finishing fully?

And what did Paul report at the end of his life in 2 Timothy 4:7?

Now, what is your seemingly impossible task, and how can you follow in Caleb-the-giant-killer's giant steps? Don't forget to jot down the first step you will take!

- *Achsah*—This ingenious daughter of Caleb possessed quickness of discernment. Recognizing that the land given to her would be useless without water, she did the right thing—she asked! And she asked the right person— her father! In a few words, pinpoint the positive trait(s) that most accurately describes Achsah's character.

What description of a wise homemaker is given in Proverbs 31:27?

How can you follow through on these three steps of diligent home management?

Step 1—*Watch*. How can you do a better job of watching over your home?

Step 2—*Improve*. What home improvements should you make around your house?

Step 3—*Ask*. How can you be more faithful in asking God and others for wisdom and support?

Cultivating a Life of Character

What a wonderful roll call of godly people who followed through on their commitments, their responsibilities, their instructions, and their word! Wouldn't you, too, dear woman after God's own heart, want your name added to the likes of Caleb and Achsah...and the Proverbs 31 Woman? The quality of faithfulness is a fruit of the Spirit (Galatians 5:23), you know. It is on display when we are walking by the Spirit, when we are walking in obedience to God, when we are living to serve God instead of ourselves. God is honored and others are blessed when you and I faithfully follow through.

Lesson 3

Setting the Scene

Judges 2:1–3:6

*A*s a writer, I try to pay attention to how other writers communicate. I'm always looking for tips and models of creative style. Well, this current portion of Scripture certainly amazed me! Why? Because of the masterful way the author of the book of Judges sets the scene for the entire book by giving us so much information (information covering hundreds of years) in so few verses! Do you want to know how he did it? In a word, by *repetition*.

In today's lesson we are treated to an overview of what is going to continue occurring during the period between Joshua's conquest of the land and the establishment of a monarchy. What you are about to read describes God's dealings with His sinful people during the period of the judges...over and over and over again! As you study through the lessons from Judges, remember that you are witnessing

21

repeated descriptions of the *unfaithfulness* of God's people and the *faithfulness* of God to come to the aid of His people. In short, Judges is a picture of man's unfaithfulness and God's faithfulness.

God's Message...

1. Read now Judges 2:1–3:6. Check here when you are finished. _____

   Judges 2:1-5—Meet the most important Person in the book of Judges! Who is He, and what was His message to the Israelites and His assessment of their behavior?

   (Just a note—Most scholars believe that "the Angel of the LORD" is a pre-incarnate appearance of the Lord Jesus Christ. Such an appearance is called a *Christophany.*)

   There is always a consequence for disobeying God. What did God say the consequence was in this instance, and what was the response of the people?

2. Judges 2:6-9—As you read these verses, what do you learn about the impact of the leadership of Joshua and his contemporaries upon God's people? And how did Joshua's leadership end?

3. Judges 2:10-15—Describe the acts of the next generation of Israelites and God's response to these acts.

4. Judges 2:16-19—Finally we witness the institution of the office of "judge." What was the role and the purpose of the judges...and how did God enable them?

Nevertheless, what was the people's general response to the leadership of the judge?

5. Judges 2:20-23—In a few words, note God's regard toward His people and the consequence of their disregard of Him and His judges.

6. Judges 3:1-6—In as few words as possible, what took place in these verses and why?

Also note the steps God's people took *away* from God and *toward* paganism.

...*and Your Heart's Response*

In the midst of repetition and overview, strong themes emerge that call for a heart response from every woman after God's own heart. Let's consider just a few of these themes.

- *Do teach your children with all diligence* (2:10). It only took one generation to lose a godly devotion. To keep this from happening, what commands did God give to parents (Deuteronomy 6:6-7)?

Looking to the New Testament, how is the command to teach your children repeated in Ephesians 6:4?

If you are a parent, what can you do on a *daily* basis to instruct your children in the Christian faith? Now, what will you do today?

- *Don't compromise with your culture* (Judges 2:11-13; 3:5-7). The Israelites allowed the surrounding pagan nations to influence them rather than holding fast to God's standards. Read 2 Corinthians 6:14-18, and then note how you can better guard against the attitude and temptations of the world.

- *Do listen to your leaders* (2:16-17). God faithfully and mercifully provided leaders for His people. And what was their response?

  God is still faithfully providing leaders for His people. What message do 1 Thessalonians 5:12-13 and Hebrews 13:7 and 17 send about listening to the leaders in your church, and how does following their advice help you cultivate a life of character?

- *Do obey the Word of God* (2:17-20; 3:4). It's obvious the Israelites in the days of the judges had a problem with obeying the commandments of the Lord. Name one area in your life where you can begin cultivating a life of character that is marked by faithful obedience.

Cultivating a Life of Character

It's been said that character is not marked by a single act, but by the multitude of decisions we make on a daily basis. The themes we've looked at here are daily decisions that you and I must make. Doing so, my dear friend, will set you apart as one who is actively seeking to cultivate godly character.

There remains yet another vital daily mark of a life of character—

- *Do thank God for the tests of life* (2:22; 3:1-2,4). God left many obstacles in the path of the Israelites...to test their faith.

  Has God left obstacles in your life—hostile people, difficult situations, baffling problems—to further develop your faith and obedience?

  Won't you pause now, look at 1 Thessalonians 5:18, and then thank God for the tests of life?

Lesson 4

Meeting the Judges

Among my favorite books (other than the Bible) are the biographies of the saints who have gone before us. That's because the stories of their lives reveal their godly character through good times and bad. The details of the trials they encountered and the lessons they learned point to how character is developed.

Today we read the biographies of three "judges" whom God raised up to deliver His people. The role of a "judge" in the book of Judges is that of a governor or officer who was a military and spiritual deliverer or liberator of God's people. The judges gave local leadership and, unlike royalty, left no successors.

Dear one, God has powerful lessons for us to learn about courage from the lives of His first three powerful judges. Let's meet them now.

God's Message...

1. Read now Judges 3:7-31. Check here when you are finished. _____

In our previous lesson we mentioned the repetitive cycle of Israel's history, which we will witness again and again in the book of Judges. Be sure you keep this repeated cycle in mind as you continue this study.

Sin—Israel did evil in the sight of the Lord.

Servitude—God gave them over to another nation.

Supplication—Israel cried out to God for help.

Salvation—God sent a deliverer, a judge.

2. Judges 3:7-11—In which verse(s) and in what words do we learn about...

...sin—

...servitude—

...supplication—

...salvation—

3. Judges 3:12-30—In which verse(s) and in what words do we learn about...

...sin—

...servitude—

...supplication—

...salvation—

4. Judges 3:31—What was the name of this third judge?

Now fill in the information needed for these three judges on the chart in the back of your book. (In some cases, not every part of your chart can be filled in.)

...and Your Heart's Response

Now for some highlights from this trio of judges!

* *Othniel*—Look again at Judges 1:12-13. What have we learned about this man of character? His abilities at war? His family ties?

From the information given in Judges 3:7-11, what was the source of Othniel's empowerment? And what were the results of this empowerment?

(It's helpful to know that "the Spirit of the LORD came upon him" is a common Old Testament expression signifying a unique act of God, which conferred power and wisdom for victory.[5] This same phrase will be used of other judges in lessons to come.)

How do the following promises from God help you, as a New Testament believer, to courageously face your own battles?

1 Corinthians 15:57—

2 Corinthians 2:14—

2 Corinthians 9:8—

Ephesians 3:20—

- *Ehud*—Othniel had a special ability as a skillful warrior. Ehud, on the other hand, had a "disability." What specific detail is given about the man Ehud in verses 12-30?

God is ready...and able...to use our unique qualities to accomplish His work. Being left-handed in Ehud's day was considered a weakness, a handicap, an abnormality. In fact, the Hebrew phrase used in Judges 3:15 for left-handed means "hindered in the right hand."[6] Do you, dear one, have some special ability...or disability...that you can present to God to be used for His purposes? Note it here...and then present it to God for His use.

What glory *He* will receive when *He* uses a perceived weakness in *you* to do a great work!

- *Shamgar*—D. L. Moody, renowned pastor of old, wrote in the margin of his Bible a list of "Weak things made strong."[7] Regarding Ehud, that weak thing made strong was a left hand, and concerning Shamgar, it was an ox-goad. What was Shamgar able to accomplish with an ox-goad, a simple implement used by peasant farmers?

Look at the "little life" of Dorcas in Acts 9:36-39. What weak or simple or "little things" about your life could you use for the Lord's service today?

*I*t is no matter how weak the weapon is if God direct and strengthen the arm. An ox-goad, when God pleases, shall do more than Goliath's sword. And sometimes He chooses to work by such unlikely means that the excellency of the power may appear to be of God.[8]

Cultivating a Life of Character

How's your "biography" shaping up, dear one? Do you desire to do great things—even great "little" things—for God? To be a woman with a heart of courage? The three judges whose biographies we've just read were common folk. Yet they possessed uncommon courage. God strengthened their weaknesses, worked through their limitations, and empowered them to do great things. To follow in their giant steps of courage, let's make a pact to cultivate courage by—

—studying God's Word (to better understand the Source of courage),

—setting aside sin (that weakens courage), and

—stepping out in faith (that exhibits courage).

Igniting a Nation

Judges 4:1-24

*D*ear woman after God's own heart, two entries from the diary of Jim Elliot, martyred by the Auca Indians, show you and me what it means to have a heart that is consumed with God and with His purposes. I want to share one now and one at the end of this thrilling lesson about another woman after God's own heart—about Deborah, a woman whose flame of passion and zeal for God was used to ignite a nation. Then let's see what "fueled" Deborah's life!

*G*od makes His ministers a flame of fire. Am I ignitable? God, deliver me from the dread asbestos of "other things." Saturate me with the oil of Thy Spirit that I may be a flame. Make me Thy fuel, Flame of God.[9]

God's Message...

1. Read now Judges 4:1-24. Check here when you are finished. _____

2. Judges 4:1-3—As we consider again the fourfold cycle of Israel's history (*sin*→ *servitude*→ *supplication*→ *salvation*), note which steps of this cycle occur in verses 1-3.

3. Judges 4:4-9—Note that Israel's "salvation" in the form of a judge occurs in a most unusual person—a woman! How does the Bible describe Deborah, and what was her relationship with the people of Israel (verse 5)?

   Who was Barak, and what was Deborah's prophecy to him? And what was Barak's response?

   (Just a note—some consider Barak to be one of the judges of Israel. However, in this study we will consider Barak, along with Caleb, in chapter 1, to be a military commander.)

4. Judges 4:10-16—Identify the participants of Israel's group effort and victory.

5. Judges 4:17-22—Now describe Jael, another key participant in Israel's triumph, and the events that took place in her tent. (See also verse 11.)

6. Judges 4:23-24—In the end, what was the outcome of Israel's efforts?

...and Your Heart's Response

This Bible study is titled *Cultivating a Life of Character*. Let's shine the spotlight on Deborah again and draw our own life lessons from her life of character.

- *Deborah, the prophetess*—A prophet was one who was "divinely inspired to communicate God's will to His people, and to disclose the future to them."[10] The term "prophetess" occurs rarely in the Bible. Look at these scriptures to learn about some of the women who prophesied, noting their names and any special details surrounding their unusual ministries.

     Exodus 15:19-21—

     2 Kings 22:11-14—

     Luke 2:22,36-38—

     Acts 21:8-9—

As we can see from these scriptures, God can...and does...use women mightily. You and I will probably not be used in the way that Deborah was, but note how we *can* be used according to the New Testament.

1 Timothy 5:9-10—

Titus 2:3-5—

Do you think leading a nation is more important than loving a family? Do you think watching over God's people is more important than watching over your own family and home? Read again 1 Timothy 5:9-10 and Titus 2:3-5, answer these questions, and give your reasoning for your answers. Then treat yourself to the encouragement of the quote that follows.

*F*or most women, their greatest impact on society is through raising godly children. If a woman is godly and if God chooses to give her children whom she raises in the nurture and admonition of the Lord, she will have a profound influence on a new generation. Men may have the outward, overt leadership, but women may have just as great an influence indirectly.[11]

• *Deborah, the wife*—Besides her remarkable use by God in Israel's history, deliverance, and salvation, how else is Deborah described in Judges 4:4?

I have a favorite quote that goes like this:

> *~ God has no greater ground*
> *for those who are unfaithful*
> *where they are. ~*

To become like Deborah—a woman used greatly by God, a woman entrusted with great responsibility, a woman given a great ground for service to the kingdom—you and I must first, if we are married, be faithful to God's instructions to us as a wife. After all, God is honored when you as a wife...

...help your husband (Genesis 2:18),

...follow your husband (Ephesians 5:22),

...respect your husband (Ephesians 5:33), and

...love your husband (Titus 2:4-5).

Note any adjustments you need to make in your role as a wife—or in your attitude toward being a wife.

* *Deborah, the judge*—There's no doubt Deborah was a great and gifted woman, an unusual woman of wisdom and influence. And as the only woman in the distinguished company of the judges, she ruled Israel with equity, dispensing righteousness and justice. What character qualities do you most desire to emulate from the life of Deborah, and how can you begin cultivating them?

Cultivating a Life of Character

Dear one, there's one more exciting "heart" characteristic in our Deborah. As commentator Herbert Lockyer describes her below, Deborah was also *Deborah, the "agitator."*[12]

> Deborah was an effective agitator who stirred up Israel's concern about its low spiritual condition....She aroused the nation from its lethargy and despair....Day after day, she excited those who gathered to hear her words of divine wisdom....

How is your passion quotient, dear one...or should I say "agitation" quotient? Is your devotion to God fearless? Passionate? Is it hot enough to ignite others? And are you bold enough to speak up and enthusiastic enough to speak forth so that others are infused with a fearless faith? Or do you need to "fire up" your fervor for the things of the Lord? Let's pray now with Jim Elliot, "God, I pray Thee, light these idle sticks of my life, that I may burn for Thee."[13]

Lesson 6

Remembering Victory

Do you know the story behind "The Star Spangled Banner"? Its words commemorate an American victory over the British in 1812. A jubilant song, its words state that the bombs bursting in air revealed that America's flag was still there. Every time we sing this song, we relive a historic event.

The Bible, too, is full of commemorative songs. We can "hear" the song Moses and his sister Miriam sang after the deliverance of Israel from Pharaoh (Exodus 15). David sang as the ark of the Lord was brought up to Jerusalem (1 Chronicles 16). Hannah rejoiced in the Lord (1 Samuel 2). Mary's song poured forth her magnificat (Luke 1). Some say Sarah "sang" the first recorded lullaby when her little Isaac was born at last (Genesis 21:6-7).

Well, tune your heart strings, precious sister! Today we are privileged to listen to a song that transmits to us these many centuries later the details of the great victory of God's people over Jabin, king of Canaan. Let's "listen in" now as this inspired bird's-eye view of Israel's battle against the Canaanites is recounted in song.

God's Message...

1. Read now Judges 5:1-31. Check here when you are finished. _____

2. Judges 5:1-5—*Praise*—To whom was Deborah and Barak's song sung (verses 2-3)?

3. Judges 5:6-8—*Past*—As Deborah and Barak reviewed the conditions before God's victory over their enemies, what is revealed about the situation in Israel?

4. Judges 5:9-18—*Participants*—This long section of Deborah's recounting of Israel's battle is a roll call of the tribes of Israel and lists those who participated in Israel's battle...and those who did not. Reread this section with this information in mind.

5. Judges 5:19-22—*Prosperity*—The God of Israel intervened on behalf of His people, setting the very forces of nature into "battle array" against the Canaanite enemies. Note the role of...

...the stars (verse 20)—

...the river of Kishon (verse 21)—

6. Judges 5:23-30—*Parallel*—Preacher and teacher D. L. Moody called verse 23 "The Do-Nothing's Curse."[14] Who was that "Do-Nothing"?

By contrast, who did "something," something great, something admirable and praiseworthy (verse 24)?

What was prophesied in Judges 4:9, and how was that prophecy fulfilled?

Although Jael's actions abused all of the conventions of hospitality of her day, she is nevertheless praised for her zeal for Israel in its battle against its oppressor. Indeed, she is celebrated and "blessed" as a heroine, a foreign woman who loved God and was an instrument in His victory over His enemies.

7. Judges 5:31—*Prayer*—Catch the beauty and the spirit of verse 31! What is the hope of this prayer from the heart and lips of Deborah and Barak?

8. With the close of Judges chapter 5, we get the final bit of information for our chart on the judges. Fill it in now.

...and Your Heart's Response

I hope you are grasping the meaning—and the joy and the triumph—of this song of remembrance. The Lord is indeed good...and His faithfulness to His people is everlasting!

Now, let's tie up some loose ends in the tapestry of Deborah's life of character. In our previous lesson, we began working our way through a list of Deborah's roles and character qualities. We admired Deborah, the prophetess, the wife, the judge, and the agitator. Now let's finish that list.

- *Deborah, the warrior*—Once Deborah was through speaking her stirring words, words of zeal and appeal as she called Israel to battle against God's foes, what did this gallant woman and judge do (Judges 4:10)?

  And what was the outcome of that battle (Judges 4:15 and 23-24)?

  Deborah's was a brave heart! But a greater issue here and now is…how do *you* stand up to the rigors of battle, to the challenges God hands *you?* Are you one who follows through? Who persists to the end? Who assists and encourages others in their battles? This is our heart response section, dear friend! How does Deborah's dauntless character inspire you to stand firm and to trust in the Lord? And what element from Deborah's life can you take into your battle?

- *Deborah, the poetess*—It was said of Julius Caesar that "he wrote with the same ability with which he fought."[15] Deborah, the warrior, went out to war. And when God gave the victory to Israel, Deborah's brimming heart spilt over in pure praise and thanksgiving. She penned a poem that exalted her *God*, that encouraged her *faith*, that encouraged her *people*...and that should encourage *your* faith, too. She, like Caesar, certainly wrote as well as she fought!

Do you have a favorite song or hymn of worship and praise that you can use to encourage your faith in trials? Write out a few of its stirring words here and briefly note how they incite you to keep on keeping on. And don't forget to share them with others who need to be encouraged!

• *Deborah, "a mother in Israel"*—We don't know if Deborah experienced motherhood or not. But we do know that Deborah arose as "a mother in Israel" (Judges 5:7). Like a mother, she watched over the spiritual well-being of God's people with maternal care, nursing their insecurities, inciting their faith, and leading them in the right direction—God's direction.

Are you a mother, dear one? As you consider this maternal characteristic in our Deborah, how can you better guide your brood? How can you point them in the good, the better, and the best direction? How can you better ignite their desire to follow God? And, if you are not a mother, how can you serve others in Deborah's motherly manner through discipling, mentoring, and modeling a life of character? Make a list now.

Cultivating a Life of Character

As I think about Deborah in this chapter from the book of Judges, one character trait seems to stand out above all others. That trait is utter humility. Deborah was a woman who only wanted to serve God and never failed to acknowledge God in everything. Her song of remembrance speaks of this over and over again.

Who was the leader of Israel? Deborah, the leader, says it was God. Who fought against Jabin? Deborah, the warrior, says it was God. Who brought about Israel's victory? Deborah, the savior of Israel, says God gave her dominion over the mighty.

Deborah wrote of the brilliance of the shining sun at its brightest. And, dear one, Deborah's career, too, was truly brilliant. Why? Because hers was a humble heart—a heart fixed on God. She served God "to the max," to the limit of her ability. And she fought for the Lord "to the max," with a song on her lips and a sword in her hand.[16] She was a rock… because of her faith in God. She was a warrior…because of her confidence in God. She was a poetess…because of a heart brimming with praise for God. She became a "mother" to her people…because of her usefulness to God.

So…how can you nurture a heart of humility? Make sure you keep a song of remembrance in your heart…a song that remembers *God's* victories on *your* behalf!

*esson 7

Facing Your Fears

Judges 6:1-40

ear, described as a feeling of uneasiness or apprehension, is not always a bad thing. For example, in the interest of our self-preservation, we as human beings are trained to fear people, places, and things that might hurt us. Even the great apostle Paul referred to his own "fears" in 1 Corinthians 2:3. Plus, the Bible speaks of "the fear of the Lord." Now, *this* kind of fear is definitely a good thing—it's a reverential respect for our Creator, which pleases the Lord and helps to lead us in the right way. We are also told in the Bible to "flee" or to fear sin. This, too, is a good thing. So then, fear can be a *good* thing.

But fear can also be a *bad* thing...if it paralyzes us into inactivity. Our lesson today brings us to a study of one man's fight against his fears and shows us how God helped him to overcome his fears and to do a mighty work for Him. Before we meet him, let's do a little groundwork.

God's Message...

1. Read now Judges 6:1-40. Check here when you are finished. _____

2. Judges 6:1-10—Consider again the fourfold cycle of
   Israel's history (*sin*➔ *servitude*➔ *supplication*➔ *salvation*)
   and note which steps of this cycle occur here and in what
   verses.

   Describe the living conditions of God's chosen people at
   this time and why they were living in this manner.

3. Judges 6:11-27—I like the description of Gideon that says
   "he appears to be the type who tends to see a glass as
   half empty rather than half full."[17] Let's meet him now.

   Gideon's call (verses 11-14)—Where do we first encounter
   Gideon, and what was he doing when the Angel of the
   Lord appeared to him?

   How did the Angel of the Lord refer to Gideon?

   What accurate knowledge of God did Gideon possess,
   but with an inaccurate conclusion?

   Gideon's hesitation (verses 15-18)—What hesitations did
   Gideon express to the Angel of the Lord about His calling

upon Gideon to save Israel? And while you're at it, note the angel's assurances to Gideon.

Gideon's response (verses 19-27)—In what ways was Gideon's positive response to the angel's message and call evidenced?

4. Judges 6:28-40—Once Gideon was convinced of his calling, he took immediate action! However, after this initial act of valor (verses 28-35), what do we find Gideon doing (verses 36-40)?

How was the patience of the Lord revealed in His dealings with His doubting servant Gideon?

...and Your Heart's Response

- *Your call*—Gideon was called to be a judge and a warrior. As women after God's own heart, you and I possess a calling from God, too. And it's a *high* calling! Read Titus 2:3-5 now and write out what your high calling from God is. And don't worry so much about whether you are married or single. Just look for the roles and character qualities that God calls us to.

Circle or star any of these ten essentials for godly living that need improvement, and purpose to do whatever you must to cultivate these godly character qualities in your life.

• *Your hesitation*—Gideon hesitated to respond to God's calling upon his life because of one basic flaw— "Gideon's language...indicates a *weak theology*"[18] (emphasis added). He had a weak theology about God's *Person*, about God's use of *people*, about God's *presence*, and about God's *power*.

Can you think of a promise from God out of His Word that you need to remember so that you can shore up any weak theology you may have regarding God's faithfulness to you? Share it here.

Gideon whined, "I am the least" (Judges 6:15). But God uses common people like you and me, as we see below.

*J*acob...was a liar.
Joseph...was a slave.
Moses...was a shepherd in exile (and a murderer!).
Gideon...was a farmer.
Jephthah...was a son of a prostitute.
Hannah...was a barren housewife.
David...was a shepherd boy and last-born of the family.
Ezra...was a scribe.
Esther...was a slave girl.
Mary...was a peasant girl.
Matthew...was a tax-collector.
Luke...was a Greek physician.
Peter...was a fisherman.[19]

Read 1 Corinthians 1:26-29 and 2 Corinthians 12:9-10. Do you agree or disagree that God's grace and provision are large enough to make up for what you may lack, and why?

• *Your response*—Is there any area of service to our great and wonderful God where you are hesitating to respond due to fear, my dear reading friend? How can the truths of God's Word and/or the example of Gideon's life help you to face and fight your fears and actively respond to God's calling?

Cultivating a Life of Character

I love Gideon, don't you? Why? Because I identify with his fearful makeup. And believe me, I hear from a *lot* of the Lord's ladies who possess the same fears I do! Let me quote from a letter I received just this week.

> My heart has been longing to lead a small group...but my insecurities are great, and I am afraid I will fail....One of the things I fear is....Can you tell how scared I am!!!

Dear friend, one sure way to face our fears is to equip and arm ourselves with the knowledge and assurance that God's Word gives us. Gideon wanted to serve God and he wanted to know God's will. No way did he want to assume leadership or rush into battle without knowing it was God's express will! So Gideon asked God for a sign (or two...or three!). He reminds me of my junior high algebra teacher who was from Missouri, the "Show-Me State." One of her teaching methods in our oral drills was to tell us, "Show me! I'm from the 'Show-Me State.'" Well, Gideon continually said to God, "Show me!" He wanted proof before he moved out to battle.

But you, my friend and sister-in-service, need not test the Lord in the ways that Gideon did, nor ask for signs, nor set out fleeces in order to gain the valuable character quality of courage. No, your sure way to cultivate courage is to cultivate your knowledge and faith in God's Word. Then you will know His will for your life. That knowledge should give you courage in facing and fighting against your fears.

Lesson 8

Living Out Your Potential

Judges 7:1–8:21

A favorite quote of mine starts out with these words: "A hero does not set out to be one.... He was simply doing what had to be done!"[20]

Gideon, the hesitant and fleece-flinging farmer we met in the previous lesson, was a man who most certainly did not set out to become a hero! However, because he trusted in God and God gloriously enabled him, he did what had to be done...and shines forth as a Bible hero for all times.

As we look further at Gideon's life and witness this simple-but-faithful man living out his potential, keep in mind 2 Corinthians 4:7, which reminds you and me that we are but weak and "earthen vessels." Therefore, the excellency of the power of God shines all the brighter as He uses us to do His work.

God's Message...

1. Read now Judges 7:1–8:21. Check here when you are finished. _____

2. Judges 7:1-8—To begin our study, look at Judges 6:33 to see what is happening.

   Also, by what other name was Gideon known (Judges 7:1)?

   As Gideon and his warriors prepared to face the Midianites, what did God say to him...and why (verse 2)?

   What was the first group to be rejected for battle...and how many were rejected (verse 3)?

   What was the Lord's next message (verse 4)?

   God devised a test. Briefly describe that test (verse 5) and the results (verse 6).

   Which group did the Lord approve...and how many made up that group (verse 7)?

3. Judges 7:9-25—When God gave Gideon the word to get ready for battle, what provision did God make for Gideon's possible fear (verse 10)?

And, sure enough, what did Gideon do (verse 11)...and what did he and his servant hear (verses 13 and 14)?

Briefly describe Gideon's battle plan and its results (verses 16-22).

4. Judges 8:1-21—How did Gideon make peace with those who complained (verses 1-3)?

The remainder of Judges 8 contains details of the defeat of two kings, Zebah and Zalmunna. Take a minute and note a few of the details that stand out to you.

...and Your Heart's Response

- *God gave the victory.* Think back through the "battle strategy" and the "battle scene" presented in these scriptures. What details make it obvious that God gave the victory?

- *God used a few rather than the many.* God reduced Gideon's forces from 32,000 to 300. Why? To parade *His* glory before all men. You see, *His* strength...not that of a massive army...delivered His people. God used, as it were, a handful of "earthen vessels" (2 Corinthians 4:7)— as well as literal earthen pots! God gave the victory in a most unusual way. Therefore God got the glory! Never would anyone miss this fact! Now, how does the outcome of the "battle strategy" and the "battle scene" illustrate 1 Corinthians 1:27-29?

- *God gave encouragement to Gideon.* Even though God had already given Gideon the assurance of absolute victory (Judges 7:7), He nevertheless strengthened Gideon one more time by giving him one more opportunity to be assured of God's power and victory (Judges 7:9-11). Write out a few of the promises from the Bible that assure you of God's power and victory in your "battles."

Remember...God did not say to Gideon, "Don't be afraid!" God said, "In case you're afraid...." Armed with God's abundant assurance, Gideon went on to live out his potential and do extraordinary things for God.

An ordinary person used *by* God is one who can do extraordinary things *for* God.[21]

Cultivating a Life of Character

How does one live out his or her potential? In the case of Gideon, *because* God gave the victory and *because* God gave encouragement to his servant and judge, Gideon emerged as a strong leader and warrior.

Gideon's start was a slow and weak one. But it can't be denied that once Gideon dived in, he was in all the way! He went into full action! And, as we've witnessed in these few lessons about Gideon, his actions bore the mark of imme- diate and complete obedience. Yes, our Gideon may have been slow to be convinced, but he certainly got the job done...and mightily! His behavior lived out the Angel of the Lord's salutation—"you mighty man of valor" (Judges 6:12). God saw something in Gideon, some potential, that we see worked out in his life. God took a fearful coward and trans- formed him into a mighty man of valor.

Now, dear woman after God's own heart, what seemingly impossible task is God asking of you so that you, too, may live out your full potential?

Lesson 9

Ending Poorly

*I*n our final glimpse of the life of Gideon-the-judge, we are saddened to spot a mass of tarnish on the sterling character of Gideon that we've carried with us from our two previous lessons. Here we learn that Gideon fathered a son through a sexual relationship outside marriage—a son who would wreak havoc both on Gideon's family and on the nation of Israel. We also see that Gideon-the-father failed to establish his family in the ways of the Lord.

What is written of Gideon here serves as a loud warning to you and me, dear one!

*P*erhaps it is easier to honour God in some courageous action in the limelight of a time of national emergency than it is to honour Him consistently in the ordinary, everyday life, which requires a different kind of courage. Gideon, who came through the test of adversity with flying colours, was not the first nor the last to be less successful in the test of prosperity.[22]

God's Message...

So far we know that Gideon had done well. True, he got off to a slow start, but once his faith was fortified, he began to fearlessly fulfill his calling as God's judge. Let's look now at the next (and final) chapter of Gideon's life—a life that began well...and ended poorly.

1. Read now Judges 8:22–9:57. Check here when you are finished. _____

2. Judges 8:22-23—What honor did the people extend to Gideon, how did he respond, and why?

3. Judges 8:24-35—Speaking of anticlimax! What confusing, unexplainable act did Gideon commit (verses 24-27), and what effect did it have on Gideon, his family, and God's people?

(It's helpful in understanding this passage to know that an ephod was a garment generally worn by the high priest of Israel and was made of costly materials, worked with gold and precious stones.)

What was the overall effect of Gideon's judgeship (verse 28)?

Detail the final facts about Gideon and his family—both the good and the bad (verses 29-32).

As occurred after the time of each of the judges, what did the Israelites do after Gideon's death (verses 33-35)?

4. Now fill in the information needed on the chart of the history of Israel's judges in the back of your book.

5. Judges 9:1-57—As you observe this disheartening chapter of the Bible, remember that this is a spiritually depressing (and depressed!) time in the history of God's people. Many scholars point to Judges 21:25 as the key verse in the book of Judges. Write out that verse here.

With this background in mind, it's no wonder that confusion often reigned...as we see in this parenthetical chapter about the ambitious Abimelech. Who was Abimelech (Judges 8:31) and what was his origin?

(It also helps to be reminded in our study of the judges of Israel that Abimelech was not a judge but a wild, rebellious usurper of leadership who caused civil war.)

After scanning through the awful details of Judges 9, write out verse 56, which is perhaps the key verse in this chapter.

...and Your Heart's Response

- Before we look at Gideon's life, consider, and write down, what Judges 9:56-57 teaches you about...

  ...those who do evil

  ...the character of God

- Fill in the blanks and compare the character of this father and son.

  _____ had no ambition to be king...but
  _____ did.

  _____ would not accept the crown...but
  _____ did.

  _____ led God's people for God...
  _____ led them away from God.

How does this comparison speak to your heart about...

...ambition?

...pride?

...character?

- There is no denying that...

    Gideon was courageous—What was the source of his courage, and how can you possess such courage yourself?

    Gideon was consecrated—He became God's servant. Where is your realm of service? Is it on the battlefront of the home, or in the church, or in the community? Please explain your answer.

    Gideon was committed—Once he was in the race, he was in all the way! Does this describe you, dear one? Or is something holding you back?

    Gideon was changed—by the transforming power of God from a farmer to a fighter and a figure of justice. Share a few changes that have occurred in your life since you became a Christian.

    Gideon was cunning—as a brilliant military strategist. What has God gifted you to do well? (And be sure to give Him thanks!)

Gideon was counted worthy—of God's Hall of Fame. What does Hebrews 11:32-33 say about Gideon? And who were his peers?

Beloved, this is God's final word about His servant Gideon. This is what was written on his tombstone by God, so to speak. So, dear one, be sure to cultivate your faith as carefully and as diligently as you cultivate your character!

Cultivating a Life of Character

As we close the curtain on this sad scene about a man of mighty valor, one lesson stands out—cultivating a life of character takes a lifetime! We as women after God's own heart can never relax in our quest for character. We must always be on guard against tarnishing our character in any way. God's reputation is at stake...and so is our family's future! Make it your aim (by God's grace!) to end well.

Responding to God

Judges 10:1-18

I once read a book titled *It Takes So Little to Be Above Average.*[23] I loved the title…and, my friend, it certainly applies to this chapter of God's Word. Here we run into two unlikely "heroes"—two average men, judges, minor characters—who simply responded to God when the call came. During the dark days of the judges and in the midst of the ongoing apostasy of God's people, these men—these average men—"arose to save Israel" (Judges 10:1).

Let's learn some positive lessons from the example of these two judges and some not-so-positive lessons from the pattern of sin the Israelites followed.

God's Message…

This chapter of the Bible has been dubbed by another as "drab reading." However, dear one, as you make your way through these next 18 verses, keep in mind the facts stated in 2 Timothy 3:16-17: "All Scripture is given by inspiration of God, and is profitable for doctrine, for reproof, for correction, for instruction in righteousness, that the man [or woman] of God may be complete, thoroughly equipped for every good work." With these words in mind, let's inspect the reigns of two more judges, who are termed "minor" judges due to the scant details concerning their lives and leadership.

1. Read now Judges 10:1-18. Check here when you are finished. _____

2. Judges 10:1-2—Who was Israel's next judge, and what is recorded about this man?

3. Judges 10:3-5—Who succeeded Tola, and what is recorded about him?

4. Judges 10:6-18—Look again at lesson 3 and write out the repeated and persistent fourfold cycle that was common in Israel's history.

How did Israel sin this time (verse 6)?

And what was the result (verse 7)?

How long did Israel's servitude last this round (verse 8)?

When God's people finally called out to Him, what was God's response (verses 10-14)?

And what was the response of the people in...

...verse 15?

...verse 16?

What was the result of these words and actions (verse 16)?

As the Israelites gathered together for war, what was their cry (verse 18)?

5. Now, fill in the information needed for the chart in the back of your book for both judges.

...and Your Heart's Response

- *Tola*—As we focus on the verbs in the two verses that describe Tola and his judgeship, we can surmise that he was a man who did what was asked of him and got the job done. If God were to write two verses about your life and your service to Him, what would they reveal about...

    ...your faithfulness to Him?

    ...your willingness to fulfill the responsibilities He has given you?

Are there things you need to do to improve the commentary on your life? List your answers here.

- *Jair*—This man, too, was available to God when called upon. He, too, got the job done. Evidently, he was a man of some wealth. And evidently his wealth did not hinder his willingness to serve God and His people.

  God's Word speaks to us about the attitude we are to have toward riches and wealth. What instruction does 1 Timothy 6:17-19 give?

  How did Lydia serve the Lord and His people with her home and wealth in Acts 16:15 and 40?

  Now, how do you view *your* possessions, and how do you use them for God's people and purposes?

- *God's people*—God's people waited ___ years (fill in from verse 8) to acknowledge their sin and respond to God. Aren't you shocked at their delay? At their compromise? At their lagging obedience! But a better use of this information is to ask ourselves, "How long does it generally take *me* to acknowledge *my* sin?" And, "Is there any sin I need to acknowledge right now?" Write out your answers now.

What do we learn about the character of God from this section of the Bible?

What does Proverbs 28:13 teach about acknowledging and not acknowledging sin?

Cultivating a Life of Character

What a contrast—the faithfulness of a few and the compromise of the many! May you and I join ranks with the few who respond to God by cultivating a life of faithfulness to Him in the midst of a compromising society. May you and I ever be quick to watch out for sin, to confess sin, to forsake sin, and to understand the seriousness of sin. Why? Because...

> *O*ur most heinous sin is not the act of wrong done, but the fact that such wrong incapacitates us from fulfilling our highest function of glorifying God.[24]

Lesson 11

Overcoming Rejection

Foreshadowing Jesus.

This is what I call a "pink passage" in the Bible—
it deals with a woman and teaches us as women. I personally mark all such passages with a pink highlighter so it
really stands out whenever I read it. And this passage today
stands out for more reasons than one!

As we comb through the facts in this chapter and turn the
spotlight on Jephthah's daughter, keep one thing in mind—
the overarching fact that God's enemies were defeated and
God used Jephthah to accomplish that victory. Regardless
of what *we* may surmise from this portion of the Bible, *God*
placed Jephthah on His roll call of the great men and women
of faith in Hebrews 11:32.

Now, onward!

65

God's Message...

1. Read now Judges 11:1-40. Check here when you are finished. _____

2. Now note the final verse of Judges 10. What was the cry of the people?

3. Judges 11:1-11—Gather a few facts about Jephthah, God's next judge, from...

   ...verse 1—

   ...verse 6—

   ...verse 11—

4. Judges 11:12-28—These verses detail the negotiations between Israel and Ammon over territory that each party believed was rightly theirs. Here we witness Jephthah, "a mighty man of valor," as a statesman seeking to avoid war. What were the results of Jephthah's efforts (verse 28)?

5. Judges 11:29-33—Three facts are revealed in these few verses. Note them from...

   ...verse 29—

   ...verses 30-31—

   ...verses 32-33—

6. Judges 11:34-40—What new person do you meet here, and what do you learn about her?

...and Your Heart's Response

- *Jephthah's victory*—What evidence do you find regarding God's part in Jephthah's victory?

I like these thoughts about Jephthah: "Jephthah, an illegitimate son of Gilead, was chased out of the country by his half brothers. He suffered as a result of another's decision and not for any wrong he had done. Yet in spite of his brothers' rejection, God used him. If you are suffering from unfair rejection, don't blame others and become discouraged. Remember how God used Jephthah despite his unjust circumstances, and realize that He is able to use you as well."[25]

What "rejection" can you now place in God's most able hands? And what steps can you take to move on in your life and in your spiritual growth?

- *Jephthah's vow*—Unfortunately, Jephthah's vow cost him in a way he did not anticipate! What does Proverbs 20:25 warn about the making of vows?

- *Jephthah's daughter*—Oh, dear! We can be sure Jephthah never imagined that his rash vow would involve his only child, his precious daughter! But this is a study about cultivating a life of character. And here we see two people living out such a life. As one has noted,

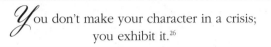

> *Y*ou don't make your character in a crisis;
> you exhibit it.[26]

What, exactly, happened here in verses 34-40? What does this passage actually describe? Scholars are evenly divided between two possible scenarios: 1) Jephthah sacrificed his daughter as a human burnt offering. 2) Jephthah's vow was fulfilled by his daughter's perpetual virginity, meaning she never married and died childless, thus leaving Jephthah with no descendants since she was his only child.

Dear reader, we just don't know what happened. But we do know that Jephthah's daughter was an outstanding example of a woman after God's own heart, a woman who revered the Lord and the sacredness and seriousness of a vow made to Him. Here's my checklist of some of her many acts of character:

✓ She rejoiced and delighted in her father's victory. She was proud of him and his accomplishment in furthering God's purposes.

✓ She joined with her father in believing that the vow must be fulfilled.

✓ She encouraged her father in his sorrow.

✓ She spent time preparing herself to follow through on her father's obedience to his vow.

✓ She possessed a corps of friends with whom she could share her time of trial.

✓ She had an impact on the nation of Israel, who did not forget her character.

Now it's your turn. Make a list of character qualities and godly traits that describe Jephthah's daughter. Then check off those you need to further cultivate so that your life, too, may be one of outstanding heroic character.

Cultivating a Life of Character

As I'm sitting here thinking back through this puzzling chapter, I can't help but notice at least five dazzling "diamonds in the dust" as I consider the character of both Jephthah and his daughter.

- They kept their word.

- They honored their vows.

- They exhibited great faith.

- They overcame great obstacles.

- They had an effect on their nation.

May these outstanding character qualities of Jephthah and his noble, courageous daughter become gems that you and I handle repeatedly as we, too, cultivate a life of character. In the words of a popular, current-day, one-minute radio counselor, "Character counts!"

Lesson 12

Dealing with Dissension

*V*ictory! That's where we left off in our last lesson! Jephthah, under the empowerment of the Spirit of the Lord (Judges 11:29), led God's people to a great victory over the Ammonites. You would think that victory would unify the fragmented tribes of Israel, wouldn't you? But as we'll see in this lesson, the opposite occurred—Jephthah's victory brought dissension rather than celebration.

Two lessons await us, dear one—

1. Understanding the causes and effects of dissension, and

2. Understanding how to deal with those causes and effects in our own heart.

Now, are you ready to learn about dealing with dissension? Then read on!

God's Message...

1. Read now Judges 12:1-15. Check here when you are finished. _____

2. Judges 12:1-7—Look again at Judges 8:1-3. Obviously, the strong northern tribe of Ephraim is having problems again. What similarities do you detect in their two complaints?

   After Jephthah defended his position, what occurred (verse 4)?

   What happened in the end, according to verse 7?

3. Judges 12:8-10—From walking alongside Jephthah, a major personality, we now move into looking at the lives and reigns of three more "minor" judges. These leaders were important to God and to His people, although little is reported about them. Who was Israel's next judge, and what is recorded about this man?

4. Judges 12:11-12—Who was Israel's next judge, and what is recorded about this man?

5. Judges 12:13-15—And who was Israel's next judge, and what is recorded about this man?

6. Now, fill in the information needed for the chart in the back of your book for these four judges.

...and Your Heart's Response

- *Jephthah*—Just look at the high cost of petty quarreling and envy among God's people! Evidently "Ephraim's newest threat was their jealousy of Jephthah's success and possibly a lust to share his spoil."[27]

What do these proverbs teach us about contention, jealousy, and envy? Also note any solutions given for avoiding these destructive sins.

Proverbs 14:30—

Proverbs 15:18—

Proverbs 26:20-21—

Proverbs 27:4—

Proverbs 29:22—

Now, how can *you* stay out of petty arguments? And how can you stay away from others who participate in or provoke them?

What steps can you take to keep a pure heart when it comes to the successes of others?

What Is Envy?

*S*hakespeare called envy "the green sickness."

Bacon admitted "it has no holidays."

Horace declared that "tyrants never invented a greater torment."

Barrie said it "is the most corroding of the vices."

Sheridan referred to it in [a] play: "There is not a passion so strongly rooted in the human heart as this."

Philip Bailey...described it as "a coat [that] comes hissing hot from hell."[28]

• *Ibzan, Elon, and Abdon*—Here again are three average men, minor characters, who were available to God, responded to God, and were used by God. What character qualities do these descriptions indicate were present in their lives? How about you? Are you, average you, ready to be used by God? Is any part of this description missing in your life? And what will you do about it?

Cultivating a Life of Character

Do you remember the beginning of our study of the book of Judges? We were forewarned that Judges is a puzzling book of the Bible. There is much here that we wonder about. And there is much here (and forthcoming!) that appalls us. God's heroes did not always exhibit exemplary behavior. But they lived and judged in spiritually dark days, as are the days when any of us chooses to do "what is right in our own eyes" instead of being a woman after God's own heart, a woman whose one desire is to fulfill all *God's* will.

However, Jephthah's life does leave us with a glimmer of light as we exit Judges 12. In the end, we see that Jephthah's leadership qualities were apparent throughout his turbulent life—a life that did not start out well. Under his leadership God's people experienced victory after victory over their enemies.

Beloved, whatever situation today finds you in—turbulent times, dissension, dark days—may your life of remarkable character shine forth and honor the Lord! Remember...

*W*e talk about our evil world,
but actually this is an ideal world
for God's purposes—for building character.[29]

Lesson 13

Receiving Guidance

Judges 13:1-25

Good and upright is the LORD;
Therefore He teaches sinners in the way.
The humble He guides in justice,
And the humble He teaches His way.
—PSALM 25:8-9

As we step into this next passage of Scripture, you'll be delighted to find it refreshing and innocent (in comparison to the darkness and confusion that has gone before!). It's the tale of a couple after God's own heart, a humble couple who wanted to do something terribly important in the right way—in God's way. They were given a major assignment from God, and they were in fear of botching it. Therefore, they desired to receive guidance from God so they could know His will.

Oh yes—this is also another "pink passage" that introduces us to another terrific woman of the Bible!

God's Message...

1. Read now Judges 13:1-25. Check here when you are finished. _____

2. Judges 13:1-7—As usual, what was the spiritual condition of the children of Israel (verse 1)?

What two people do we meet in verse 2, and what details about their lives are given?

What startling occurrence and announcement was made in verses 3-5? Also, what unusual instructions were given, and why would this child be so important?

3. Judges 13:8-23—What was the essence of Manoah's prayer in verse 8, and how did God answer his request (verse 9)?

Briefly describe what happened in...

...verses 9-12—

...verses 13-14—

...verses 15-21—

...verses 22-23—

4. Judges 13:24-25—At last a baby is born to this childless couple! Who was he, and what do you learn about God's activity in his life?

...and Your Heart's Response

• *The Nazirite vow*—Samson's beginning was remarkably different from that of any other judge. It came in a miraculous announcement and with specific instructions: Samson was to be "a Nazirite to God from the womb" (verse 5), which meant his mother was also to take upon herself a Nazirite vow until the child was born. The Nazirite (meaning *one separated*) was a person who was separated completely unto the Lord. Read Numbers 6:2-8 and briefly note the three restrictions that were included in the Nazirite vow:

> Restriction 1 (verse 3) —
> Restriction 2 (verse 5) —
> Restriction 3 (verse 6) —

Just for fun, note these other mothers who adhered to the Nazirite vow and the names of their famous sons:

> Hannah in 1 Samuel 1:11,20—
> Elizabeth in Luke 1:13-15,60—

• *Manoah's wife*—We find in Manoah's wife a *woman* of true character. How is her character revealed in these three basic areas of life?

> God/worship—

> Marriage/wife—

Family/parenting—

- *Manoah*—We find in Manoah a *man* of true character. How is his character revealed in these three basic areas of life?

    God/worship—

    Marriage/husband—

    Family/parenting—

After admiring the shining character traits of both Manoah and his wife, note one character quality you wish to adopt from their examples and cultivate in your own relationship with

    God/worship—

    Marriage/wife—

    Family/parenting—

- *The Angel of the Lord*—This wondrous appearance was a divine being sent from God or an actual pre-incarnate appearance of Jesus Christ. When this dear couple asked, "What is your name?" (verse 17), what did the angel say (verse 18)?

What does Proverbs 31:30 say about a woman's attitude toward God?

How did Manoah's wife and her husband exhibit their fear of the Lord?

How can you fine-tune your attitude toward God and your reverence toward Him and your worship of Him?

- *Samson*—Keep in mind as we learn more about Samson that the Nazirite vow, a vow that set him apart for God's service, was to be observed throughout his life. That meant that Samson was not to eat or drink anything from the grapevine, nor cut his hair, nor touch any dead thing.

Cultivating a Life of Character

Dear one, our character begins with our faith. Manoah's wife asked no questions, requested no signs, and showed no hint of doubt. She responded with the rare and precious silence of belief.

Character also seeks the guidance of God. Why don't you take a page out of this outstanding-but-simple couple's life and earnestly seek God's guidance for the many decisions that you must make? God guides the humble and teaches them His way!

Lesson 14

Fulfilling a Promise

Judges 14:1–15:20

Didn't you love our last lesson?! What an out-standing couple of character God chose in Manoah and his wife to bring His next judge into the world. Their list of virtues and exemplary traits is long. Like Elizabeth and Zacharias (Luke 1:6), this couple certainly found favor with God.

Mr. and Mrs. Manoah may have shared many wonderful years as they raised and enjoyed their long-awaited son. Unfortunately, however, something that began so well—with two miraculous visits from the angel of Jehovah—did not continue in that direction.

As you read this next puzzling portion of the Bible, remember that these events took place during a time when confusion reigned. Also remember that "all the judges were individualists; most of them had their flaws of character.

Nevertheless, it must be agreed that in a group of unique individuals, Samson was in a category all his own."[30]

Despite the dismal details and foolish escapades that account for most of Samson's service as a judge for God's people, there is one dazzling light that shines forth out of the mysterious mire—God was at work, in spite of His vessel, to fulfill His promise to Samson's mother (Judges 13:5).

God's Message...

1. Read now Judges 14:1–15:20. Check here when you are finished. _____

   Then copy God's final statement from Judges 13:5 to see how God is fulfilling a promise in these chapters.

2. Judges 14:1-20—In the first section of chapter 14 (verses 1-4), Samson comes of age and desires a wife. Describe the details of these verses and the conclusion of verse 4.

   Look now at verses 5-14. What act did the Spirit of the Lord empower Samson to perform (verse 6)? Also, as Samson boasted, what did he pose to the Philistines (verses 12-13)?

In verses 15-20, how did the Philistines use Samson's Philistine wife against him (verse 15)? What were the results (verses 19-20)?

3. Judges 15:1-20—As briefly as possible, recount the scene in...

...verses 1-2—

...verses 3-6—

...verses 7-8—

...verses 9-13—

...verses 14-19—

...verse 20—

4. One of the remarkable facts about Samson's judgeship is that nowhere does he have one single soldier at his side, let alone an army. Instead, we read of God's personal support and enablement of this lone man-of-the-hour. What do you learn about God's assistance to Samson in...

...Judges 14:6—

...Judges 14:19—

...Judges 15:14—

...Judges 15:18-19—

5. Now, fill in the information about the judge on the chart on pages 142-43.

...and Your Heart's Response

- *The Philistines*—From Jephthah's day until the time of David, the Philistines were a constant threat to Israel. Not only were they fierce warriors, but they outnumbered Israel and possessed superior tactical expertise and technology. Because of the advantages the Philistines had over them, the Israelites apathetically accepted servitude.

   Beloved, none of this should have mattered! Why? Because *God* was fighting for Israel!

   Can you name any "enemies," any overwhelming odds, any outside pressures that you may be apathetically accepting without a fight? In what ways has God promised you sure victory? And how can you begin to look to God to aid you in victory?

- *Samson*—As you can see, Samson was a prankster, a boaster, and a man given to sensuality. His God-given physical strength was wasted on practical jokes, bragging, brawling, and loose living. Samson treated his life like a game. His sad tale shows us the importance of identifying personal weaknesses and setting about to deal with them. Regardless of our godly heritage and our God-given abilities, a single unguarded weakness can destroy everything that we are striving to build. Can you point to any such weakness in your character at this time? Draw up a plan for shoring up that weak area.

- *The Spirit of the Lord*—It's obvious that God used Samson, a man of inconsistent and faulty character. Even though Samson yielded to pressure and was so often governed by senselessness and sensuality, God still worked to fulfill His purposes and His promise to begin to deliver Israel from its enemies.

In spite of the weakness in His man Samson, God brought about His victory over His enemies. In spite of the apathetic nature of Israel, God used one man—even a faulty, weak, foolish man—to begin delivering Israel from the yoke of the Philistines. What He has promised, He will perform!

What has God promised you from His Word that you need to count on Him to fulfill...in His time? Share briefly here.

Cultivating a Life of Character

As someone has quipped,

> The loose character
> usually winds up
> in a tight place.

True...Samson lacked wisdom and discipline and true dedication. He treated his privileges lightly. He misused his God-given abilities and blessings. He was controlled by sensuality. And he ended up in many tight places!

But God fulfilled His promise and used Samson due to his faith (Hebrews 11:32) and in spite of his mistakes! Take heart, dear one! God can use us, too!

Lesson 15

Ending Well

Judges 16:1-31

> *E*very human being is intended to have a character
> of his own; to be what no other is, and to do what
> no other can do.[31]

oday, my friend, we're finally able to see what
that "thing" is that Samson was to be and to do.

As you read and study today's lesson, take heart in the fact
that it is never too late to turn to God. It is never too late to
ask God to help us do what we are supposed to do.

God's Message...

1. Read now Judges 16:1-31. Check here when you are finished. _____

2. Judges 16:1-3—What moral weakness did Samson exhibit (verse 1)?

And what great feat of physical strength did he exhibit (verses 2-3)?

3. Judges 16:4-22—What new person is introduced, and how did the Philistines set about to use her (verses 4-5)?

Fill in the details of the following scenes:

Scene 1—Verses 6-9
Delilah asked:

Samson answered:

The scene unfolds:

Scene 2—Verses 10-12
Delilah asked:

Samson answered:

The scene unfolds:

Scene 3—Verses 13-14
Delilah asked:

Samson answered:

The scene unfolds:

<u>Scene 4—Verses 15-22</u>

Delilah asked:

Samson answered:

The scene unfolds:

4. Judges 16:23-31—<u>The Final Act</u>

The scene (verses 23-27):

The purpose (verses 23-24):

The prayer (verse 28):

The finale (verses 29-31):

...and Your Heart's Response

- No mother ever names her daughter Delilah! What lessons do you learn as a woman from the behavior of Delilah? Name at least three.

- What lessons do you learn from Samson's behavior...

...in verses 1-22?

...in verses 23-31?

• Samson's name is hung forever, so to speak, in God's hall
  of great men and women of faith. Read it now in
  Hebrews 11:32. What does this say about the faith and
  feats of this judge Samson?

• How did Samson live out this saying: "The longer we
  remain in tempting situations, the more likely we are to
  succumb"?[32] And, can you point to any area in your life
  where you are living too close to the edge?

• How did Samson live out this saying: "We are never in a
  place where God can't hear our prayers"?[33] And do you
  perhaps need to call out to the Lord? Remember, it is
  never too late to end well!

Cultivating a Life of Character

As we pause here to consider the cultivation of our own
character, we can't help but note the contradictory elements
in Samson's character.

He was a judge in Israel, yet his life story centered on his dubious relationships with Philistine women.

His unshorn locks denoted a Nazirite consecrated to God, yet his chief aim was to please himself.

He possessed great strength of body, yet lacked strength of character.

Thankfully, however, the closing scene of Samson's frivolous, wasted life shows you and me the power of the greatest character quality of all—a dependence upon God. Although Samson's beginning was weak, his ending was strong...when he turned to God. What a wonderful lesson God has for us here as women after His own heart, as women who desire to fulfill all His will. And that lesson is that it's never too late...

>...to turn to God.
>...to repent of our sinful ways.
>...to cry out for God's help.
>...to end well.

Beloved, the ultimate testimony of character is not where you start, but where you finish.

*L*esson 16

Worshiping the Wrong Way

*W*hy…oh, why…oh, why?!

These are the cries of my confused heart as I read these three awful chapters of the book of Judges! (And I'll caution you—there are two more to follow!) Perhaps the label on this lesson should read:

WARNING! WHAT YOU ARE ABOUT TO READ
CONTAINS DISTURBING INFORMATION!

(And, as my husband just reminded me, it's not unlike information you'll find on the front page of many present-day newspapers.)

As we wade through the mire of these next two lessons, keep two things in mind:

90

✓ "All Scripture is given by inspiration of God, and is profitable for doctrine, for reproof, for correction, for instruction in righteousness, that the man [or woman] of God may be complete, thoroughly equipped for every good work" (2 Timothy 3:16-17).

✓ God's Word tells the truth—the Bible does not gloss over or pass over the details—both the good and the bad—that fill the lives and the history of His people.

God's Message...

1. Read now Judges 17:1-13. Check here when you are finished. _____

Write out verse 6 here. Keep in mind that this verse (and Judges 21:25) is the key verse to understanding the book of Judges. It is also the key to understanding the sordid events and conditions of God's people that are exposed in the final five chapters of Judges.

As someone has remarked about the truth taught in this verse and in this book of the Bible,

> *E*very man did that which was right in his own eyes, and then they soon did that which was evil in the sight of God.[34]

What part did the love of money play in the setting up of a false worship?

2. Read now Judges 18:1-31. Check here when you are finished. _____

In as few words as possible (fewer than ten), note the events that indicated the downward spiral created by departing from the will of God concerning worship in...

...verses 1-13—

...verses 14-26—

...verses 27-31—

3. Read now Judges 19:1-30. Check here when you are finished. _____

Once again, in as few words as possible, summarize the events of verses 1-29—

While we witness the dark and unutterable shameless-ness of God's people and priests, we also behold a glimmer of light in the people's response and *re*action to the Levite's action. What was their response in verse 30?

...and Your Heart's Response

I know my head is spinning and my heart is hurting. As I'm searching for a way to focus on application from these chapters to our own hearts, I want us to first note the major teaching and events in each chapter and then make some general applications.

- Judges 17—A Levite was supposed to be a man who stood in a special relationship to God. As one of the twelve tribes that made up the Israelite people, the Levites were responsible to lead the people in the worship activities prescribed by the law of Moses. Obviously the religious practices and worship of the Israelites had broken down to the point of moral degradation and confusion. In essence, they were making up their own rules for worship. They were worshiping the wrong way!

- Judges 18—Here we witness the consequences of the continued sin of the Danites (another of the twelve tribes of Israel). What was their sin? The Danites had failed to trust God to help them drive out the people from the land that had been allotted to them. Therefore, they became contaminated by contact with the religions of the people around them. This led to the utter neglect of the law as given by Moses and to making up their own rules for worship. In other words, this led to worshiping the wrong way!

- Judges 19—Note two things from this chapter: 1) the degrading depth of the downward slide in the moral sense of the Israelites, and 2) a glimmer of a moral sense still remaining in the people.

- Now, let's draw some application for our lives from these chapters.

As you think about these scenes, how important is the study of God's Word to our conduct and to worshiping... the right way, in the way prescribed by God in His Word?

What fresh commitments do you need to make in your personal study of the Bible?

Cultivating a Life of Character

Beloved, God's Word lists ten character qualities that He desires you and me to cultivate as His women (Titus 2:3-5). The importance of developing a heart that worships God in the right way is revealed by the character quality He places as Number One on His list: Godliness. Holiness. Behavior that properly fits a woman who has a relationship with God. As one translation reads, God wants us "to behave as becomes the worship of God."[35]

The cultivation of a life of character begins right here— with our worship. When we worship properly, we behave properly...which glorifies God and honors His Word (Titus 2:5). Let's make a lifetime commitment to worship the Lord—His way!—and magnify Him together.

Reviewing Judges

Oh, how I dislike asking you to spend yet another day wallowing in the godless escapades of God's people! Keep in mind, though, as you read and as we close out our study that these two lessons (covering the final chapters of the book of Judges) provide an appendix for this book of the Bible. They record for us God's commentary on the lifestyle of His people as they chose to live their lives apart from Him. You'll not find many godly character qualities here!

God's Message...

1. Read now Judges 20:1-48. Check here when you are finished. _____

95

2. Again, what do these verses tell us about the condition of the nation of Israel during the time of the judges?

Judges 17:6—

Judges 21:25—

3. In as few words as possible, summarize the events of...

...verses 1-17—

...verses 18-48—

4. Read now Judges 21:1-25. Check here when you are finished. _____

Once again, in as few words as possible, summarize the events of...

...verses 1-7—

...verses 8-25—

...and Your Heart's Response

In this final section of our final lesson on the book of Judges, I want us to review the highlights of this confusing book of the Bible and seek to take their brilliance away with us.

• First, let's review the bright spots in the book of Judges. I wrote these words in our opening lesson:

Before we inspect the portraits of the men and women who fill the pages of these two historical books of the Old Testament, and before we make our way through the good, the bad, and the ugly details of both Judges and Ruth, here are a few gems you can look forward to discovering along the way:

> The constant faithfulness of God
> The forgiveness and grace of God
> The power and repeated deliverance of God
> The redeeming work of God
> The raising up of a variety of unlikely heroes
>   by God

God, dear one, is the true "star" in the sad tales told of His unlikely heroes. What aspect of God's character and His relationship with His people meant the most to you as you studied Judges, and why?

- Next let's review the book of Judges. Hopefully, you will find *The Acrostic Bible* summary most helpful—

Chapter	Acrostic
1	**T** erritories Israel left unconquered
2	**H** ow God tested Israel
3	**E** hud slays Moab's king
4	**J** abin overcome by Deborah
5	**U** plifting song of Deborah
6	**D** etermination via Gideon's fleece
7	**G** ideon's army routs Midianites
8	**E** phod causes Gideon's downfall
9	**S** hechemites make Abimelech king
10	**O** ppression by the Ammonites
11	**F** ighting Jephthah subdues Ammonites
12	**G** ileadites overcome the Ephraimites
13	**O** ppression by the Philistines
14	**D** eceit over Samson's riddle
15	**S** amson kills thousand Philistines
16	**P** hilistines find Samson's secret
17	**E** phraimite hires own priest
18	**O** ffenses committed by Danites
19	**P** erversion of Levite's concubine
20	**L** evite's vengeance on Benjamites
21	**E** xistence of Benjamin assured[36]

Look now at the information you recorded on the chart in the back of this book for the judges. Pick your two favorite judges and tell why.

- Finally, review your lessons and pick three overriding lessons you learned about character from your study of the book of Judges and the lives of the judges.

Lesson 1—

Lesson 2—

Lesson 3—

Cultivating a Life of Character

I'm thrilled that you, dear sister after God's own heart, have made it this far—all the way through the book of Judges! As we walk away from this study in character, it seems fitting to focus on God's grace—God's *amazing* grace!

✓ God's amazing grace is displayed in the deliverance of His sinning people time and time again through the leadership of His judges.

✓ God's amazing grace is traced throughout the book of Judges as human failure was often overruled by the hand of God.

✓ God's amazing grace is evidenced by the inclusion of men and women of great faith who were mixed among the faithless. As one has noted, "Grace forgives and forgets the failures and extols the faith."[37]

Thank God now for His amazing grace in *your* life!

Lesson 18

Handling Life's Losses

Ruth 1:1-10

In my A Woman After God's Own Heart seminar, I give the ladies who are present an assignment. I ask them to write down their age. Then I ask them to write down how old they will be in ten years. Finally, I ask them to project what will probably transpire in their lives during that next decade.

Too well do I remember my own answers at the time when I first did this exercise myself. On my list I noted that I would probably lose both of my parents...and my husband's as well. Also the probability that both of my children, my two daughters, would marry appeared on the page.

Well, dear one, I have suffered *many* losses in the past decade of my life. Some were on that list...and others were not—indeed, never even dreamed of!

As I'm sitting here this minute studying and creating this lesson, God is teaching me about how to handle the losses you and I will surely suffer in life. For indeed, the issue is never *if* you and I will suffer loss, but *when!*

Let's look now to a trio of widows and learn from them about handling life's losses. (Also note that these losses occurred over a ten-year period!)

God's Message...

1. Read now Ruth 1:1-10. Check here when you are finished. _____

2. Who are the six people mentioned in this passage who made up a family unit? Record what you learn about them here.

3. How did they come to be in Moab (verse 1)?

4. What good thing happened to this little family (verse 4)?

   And what bad thing happened to them (verse 5)?

5. What solution did Naomi come up with for her demise, and why (verse 6)?

...and Your Heart's Response

Before we move on to our heart's response, let's do a little "housekeeping" on the book of Ruth.

The author—It is uncertain who wrote this book of the Bible, but it was obviously someone who knew the times and was familiar with the rural culture of Bethlehem and the customs of the day.

The time—This captivating pastoral love story is set in stark contrast against the dark period of strife and confusion that existed during the days of the judges. Keep in mind that the events of the four chapters that comprise the book of Ruth probably occurred during the last half of the book of Judges or toward the later years of the life of Samuel, sometime around the tenth century B.C.

The place—Moab is mentioned, a land east of the Dead Sea. Once God's twosome of women left Moab, Bethlehem became the scene for the remainder of the book of Ruth.

The theme—The book of Ruth is about the "kinsman redeemer." Ruth possessed a relative through Naomi who came to her and Naomi's rescue in their plight. Ruth had a human kinsman redeemer, but behind her story the Lord's redeeming work in her life is on display.

The key verse—Write out Ruth 1:16 here, the verse that tells us of Ruth's undying loyalty not only to Naomi, but to Naomi's God, the God of Israel.

The book—The small-but-mighty book of Ruth forms a bridge between the time when there was no king in Israel and the time when there would be a king in Israel. Ruth, a Moabitess, a Gentile, was rewarded for her loyalty by becoming the great-grandmother of King David, the line through which Jesus Christ would come into the world!

• Now think about the many losses suffered by the folks in these few verses and jot them down.

Then write down a list of your losses.

Rather than remain in the land of their affliction, this band of widows made some hard decisions and took action to handle their losses and to better their lives. What actions did they take?

Are there any decisions you need to make and/or any actions you need to take to better handle your situation?

• What character qualities do you observe here in...

...Ruth?

...Naomi?

Before we move on, read the tribute on the next page...

Tribute to Naomi

*A*ll Ruth knew about the God of Israel was learned from the manner in which Naomi had responded to Him after the deaths of her husband and sons. But this observation was enough for Ruth to avow that "Your God will be my God." Wow! Naomi's reaction to her tragedy had actually drawn this young Gentile woman to want to know God....When life got bitter, Naomi had a choice. She could become bitter, or she could trust God. Naomi made the right choice, and her life drew others to God....Because Naomi responded as she did, the name Ruth appears in the genealogy of Jesus Christ.[38]

Cultivating a Life of Character

As I ponder these two women, words of character rush to mind. Words like courage, resolve, acceptance, trust, faith, valiance.... (I'm sure you can think of more!)

But the overwhelming lesson from the lives of these two sufferers along life's journey is *how* they realistically handled their losses. We all know that the diamond cannot be polished without friction. And, dear one, neither can the child of God be perfected without trials. Take these principles to heart as you further cultivate your own life of character:

- They accepted their loss.
- They determined to do something about their loss.
- They acted on facts, not emotion.
- They made a decision.
- They considered the needs of one another.
- They acted on their decision.

Lesson 19

Coming Home

As a native Oklahoman, I have often visited the original bronze statue that was used as the model for the famous sculpture of "The Pioneer Woman" in Ponca City, Oklahoma. Anyone who has ever peered into the hardened-yet-hopeful face of this gallant woman with babes in tow and a Bible under her arm cannot help but be moved, stirred, challenged, and convicted.

Well, my dear precious "pioneer woman," today you and I are privileged to peer into the hardened-yet-hopeful heart of yet another woman—Naomi—who moved down her own hard road toward the only hope that appeared on her horizon—home. Expect to have your heart moved, stirred, challenged, and convicted!

God's Message...

1. Read now Ruth 1:11-22. Check here when you are finished. _____ Also revisit Ruth 1:6-10.

2. *Consideration*—How did Naomi show her consideration for her young daughters-in-law (verses 8-15)?

   And how did her daughters-in-law show their consideration for their mother-in-law (verses 7 and 10)?

3. *Choices*—In the end, what choices did Naomi make (verses 7 and 18)?

   And Orpah (verses 14-15)?

   And Ruth (verses 14-18)?

4. *Coming home*—Describe Naomi and Ruth's homecoming (verses 19-22):

   The place—

   The greeting—

   The response—

   The season—

...and Your Heart's Response

- *Consideration*—Are you wondering what the dialogue between Naomi and her two daughters-in-law was all about? The law of Moses stated that younger sons could marry the widows of their deceased brothers (Deuteronomy 25:5-10). In Naomi's case, there were no younger sons. She was explaining that if these two young women returned with her to Israel, they probably would never remarry and have a family.

  Naomi was thinking more of her daughters-in-law than of herself. Explain how your heart attitude of consideration does or does not match up to Naomi's in your...

  ...relationships in general?

  ...relationships with your family members?

  ...relationships with your in-laws?

  List several ways you can be more considerate of others and walk in the character of Naomi. What will you do today?

- *Choices*—Choices determine destiny, and we find this to be true in two heathen women.

  What was at the heart of Orpah's choice (verse 15)?

And what was at the heart of Ruth's choice (verse 16)?

Dear reader, have *you* yet turned to the Lord, to the same God Ruth chose to follow? Please explain.

Ruth's choice was demonstrated by action—she packed up and left her family and her country...and her heathen gods! How has your choice to follow after God with your whole heart been evidenced by action? After you answer, reflect on the thoughts that follow.

> $\mathcal{W}$e cannot drift into grace....There is no escape from a personal decision. Orpah made her decision, and going back to her gods, sank into oblivion. Ruth's decision was totally different. She reached a spiritual crisis and became, in turn, the ancestress of our blessed Lord.[39]

- *Character*—Choices also reveal character. What character qualities do you observe here in...

  ...Ruth?

  ...Naomi?

  ...Orpah?

- *Coming home—Naomi* means "pleasant" and *Mara* means "bitter." The events that transpired in Naomi's life while in Moab had evidently brought her such grief that she could no longer think of bearing the name Naomi.

In our last lesson we considered life's losses. Thinking back on your answers, can you relate to Naomi's loss of joy? To her grief? Take a minute to remember and to relate. Jot down a word of testimony.

"The LORD has brought me home again empty....the Almighty has afflicted me." While these words look harsh on paper, they reveal a measure of Naomi's understanding and appreciation of God. Naomi knew in her heart that the losses of her life could be traced ultimately to God's sovereign will. Naomi acknowledged that her poverty was the result of God's providential dealings in her life. Although "empty," Naomi thankfully recognized that the Lord had brought her home.

Think again of your own losses. How do dear Naomi's heart for God and understanding of His workings help you to view those losses in the light of God's sovereign will for your life?

Cultivating a Life of Character

In our fast-paced, fast-track society, we are used to phrases like "Move with the movers!" "Get in or get out!" "Go for it!" "Reach for the top!" Yet here we meet in Naomi a woman who willingly went backwards.

Was Naomi's return home a step backwards or a step forward? In Naomi's case going home was definitely a step forward. Why? In Bethlehem there was food. There were friends. There were relatives who might take pity on her. And there was the true worship of the true God. To move forward in her life Naomi had to go back to the land of her beginnings.

Do you, my friend, perhaps need to return to the land of your beginnings, to "come home" to God? By that I mean, do you perhaps need to return to church? To return to your first love? To pick up your Bible and begin again to read God's precious Word so that your soul can be stirred afresh? To kneel in prayer and begin to nurture your prayer life all over again? To ask forgiveness from another or from God, so that you can revel once again in the joy of your salvation? To make a move away from practices that are weighing you down and holding you back? To spend less time with people who mock your beliefs and more time with those who build you up in your faith and encourage your relationship with God?

Sometimes the first step toward recultivating a life of character is in actuality a step backwards.

Coming to the Rescue

Ruth 2:1-16

*H*ave you ever felt like you just *happened* to be in the right place at the right time? Today we witness just such a situation of God's guidance and care for His two widowed women, Naomi and Ruth. True, each of these women had made a hard choice...but now their hard choices began to pay off and to "reap" benefits (quite literally, as you'll soon see!) as God began to open the windows of heaven and to pour out His blessings upon them.

Naomi chose to return to the land of God's people and to the place where worship of the true God occurred. And Ruth chose to go with her, declaring her faith in these now eternally famous words, "Your people shall be my people, and your God, my God" (Ruth 1:16).

Beloved, it is true that if our circumstances find us in God, we shall find God in all our circumstances!

God's Message...

1. Read now Ruth 2:1-16. Check here when you are finished. _____

2. Ruth 2:1-3—Whom do we meet in verse 1, and how is he described?

   What "happened" when Ruth went out to glean in the fields, and, again, how is the new man in the book of Ruth described (verse 3)?

3. Ruth 2:4-16—Describe the events that took place in...

   ...verses 4-7—

   ...verses 8-11—

   ...verses 12-16—

...and Your Heart's Response

- What character qualities do you observe here in...

   ...Ruth?

...Boaz? (I've left a large space because this man's list of character qualities is long...and will continue to grow throughout the book of Ruth! What a guy!)

* Write out at least one way you can emulate Ruth's character today. After making your own notes, enjoy the notes below written about Ruth's character.

The Homecoming...

...of Naomi and Ruth was to poverty, and they were faced by very practical problems. These were rendered more difficult by the fact that Ruth was a Moabitess. Yet, she it was who faced the fight, and went forth as a gleaner to gather what would suffice for immediate sustenance.[40]

* What had Boaz heard about Ruth's character, and what are others hearing about yours?

* Write out at least three ways you can emulate Boaz's kindness and generosity today.

Boaz is described by God in this chapter as Ruth's "kinsman" through her dead father-in-law and husband. Remember that the "kinsman redeemer" was one who came to the rescue. We'll see more of the role of kinsman redeemer lived out in the lessons to come. But for now be sure and note how Boaz came to the rescue of two destitute, bereft, poverty-stricken widows.

Cultivating a Life of Character

Have you been blessed by even our brief study of the book of Ruth? It's been said of this book of the Bible that "what Venus is to statuary and the Mona Lisa is to paintings, Ruth is to literature." Indeed, it's been called "the loveliest, complete work on a small scale."[41] I know for me I've already made one *giant* decision! I'm just asking God for the grace (and the energy!) to follow through on it!

As we leave these beautiful verses about two of God's beautiful people of character—one a foreigner, a widow without work and vulnerable, and the other a wealthy landowner and aging bachelor—there are at least two priceless lessons we simply must take along with us.

The first is the fact that *God guides* our life. "It was a coincidence! It just happened! It was pure luck!" How many times have you heard others describe some incident in their lives or their day with words like these? (And how many times have you said or thought words like these yourself?!) Dear one, you and I must eliminate all such thoughts and words! Why? Because God guides His people. That's that! Period! In Ruth and Boaz we have a perfect example of such guidance—God led Ruth to "happen upon" the specific field of Boaz! God guides you and me in the same way.

*T*here are no accidents in the life of faith. In its music, the accidentals perfect the harmony.[42]

The second lesson we as women after God's own heart can take to heart is the fact that *God provides*. Again, God guided Ruth to the field of Boaz...who just happened (there's that word again!) to be related to Naomi...who just happened to be a wealthy man...who just happened to be a man of godly character...who just happened to spot the hard-working Ruth, inquire about her, and provide for her and her mother-in-law.

Dear one, as God's child, you, too, have the promise of God's guidance and God's provision. May we ever take heart in the truth of the blessing Boaz spoke to Ruth:

> The LORD repay your work,
> and a full reward be given you
> by the LORD God of Israel,
> under whose wings you have come for refuge.

Forging a Friendship

Ruth 2:17-23

Meet the original "odd couple"! Meet Naomi and Ruth!

Yes, that's right. There's no way these two women should have ever forged a friendship. Naomi was old; Ruth was young. Naomi was one of God's people; Ruth was from a pagan people. There were most definitely cultural differences between these two women, not to mention language barriers. Plus...they were in-laws!

Yet both were widows. Both were struggling to survive. And both were committed to God and sought to honor Him with their lives.

Let's look at the recipe of their relationship and learn from Naomi and Ruth how to forge a friendship.

God's Message...

1. Read now Ruth 2:17-23. Check here when you are finished. _____

2. As you think back through Ruth 2:1-16 and then add verses 17 and 18 to it, what portrait regarding Ruth's character emerges?

3. What question did Naomi ask of Ruth in verse 19 when she saw the size of her day's gleanings (which, by the way, weighed in at about 30 to 40 pounds!)?

   When Naomi heard Ruth's reply (verse 19), what was her response (verse 20)?

   Also how did Naomi describe Boaz (verse 20)?

   What advice did Naomi then give Ruth (verse 22)?

4. This section ends in verse 23 as it began in verse 17. For the duration of barley and wheat harvest (approximately two months), what was the pattern of Ruth's days?

...and Your Heart's Response

- Take a few minutes and write out a paragraph or two that describe the relationship between Ruth and Naomi.

- Now describe the relationship between two cousins, Elizabeth and Mary, in Luke 1:39-56.

What was their relationship centered on?

And what did they talk about?

How did they encourage one another?

- Look now at Titus 2:3-5 and describe the relationship older and younger women are supposed to enjoy. What is...

...the role of the older woman?

...the role of the younger woman?

How do you see this lived out between Naomi and Ruth?

• What character qualities do you observe here in...

...Ruth?

...Naomi?

...Boaz?

• Now, dear one, how about you? Are you a Naomi or a Ruth? Are you older or younger? Are you the mother-in-law or the daughter-in-law? God is speaking to each and every woman through the sweet relationship enjoyed by Naomi and Ruth.

What must you do to nurture the heart of a Naomi? Or, put another way, what are you doing to forge friendships with younger women so that you might help form (and forge!) their lives for Christ?

What must you do to nurture the heart of a Ruth? Or, put another way, in what ways are you seeking out and submitting yourself to older Christian women to be taught and mentored?

Is there anything you can do today to cultivate the patience and concern an "older woman" should have, or the humble, teachable spirit a "younger woman" should have?

Cultivating a Life of Character

Dear woman after God's own heart (and mother-in-law after God's own heart and daughter-in-law after God's own heart), God has a loud and clear message for us here in the beautiful friendship of Naomi and Ruth.

If you have a mother-in-law or a daughter-in-law, you must do whatever it takes to nurture that relationship so that a friendship can be forged. It will take prayer, humility, sacrifice, and love to accomplish this. I love it when women genuinely and affectionately refer to each other as "my mother-in-love" and "my daughter-in-love." Our role as a member of a family is to love, honor, respect, and help one another. Therefore, all criticism must be put away and a heart of love put on in its place (Colossians 3:12-14). Then a friendship can be forged. And that, dear one, is the goal.

Lesson 22

Building Trust

Ruth 3:1-6

aution! What you are about to read in this lesson may seem to contain strange information! However, as you study from Ruth 3, keep in mind that the events presented here (and in our next lesson) are simply ancient Jewish customs. These practices have to do with finding a mate, with declaring intent, availability, and admiration, and with carrying on the lineage of a family through a "kinsman redeemer."

For now we want to look a little deeper into this touching and tender scene between a mother-in-law and her daughter-in-law, between an older woman and a younger woman, between a woman with answers and advice and a woman who listened to answers and heeded advice—between Naomi and Ruth.

These two precious widows have been through months (maybe even years!) of difficulty together. Indeed, their mutual problems and mutual trust in God pressed them into a friendship marked by the highest levels of trust in one another. Their friendship lives out these words—

The Glory of Friendship

The glory of friendship is not the outstretched hand, nor the kindly smile, nor the joy of companionship; it is the spiritual inspiration that comes to one when she discovers that someone else believes in her and is willing to trust her with her friendship.[43]

God's Message...

1. Read now Ruth 3:1-6. Check here when you are finished.

____

2. In Ruth 2:2, Ruth took the initiative to care for Naomi. What did Ruth suggest?

Now in Ruth 3:1-2, Naomi took the initiative to care for Ruth. What did Naomi suggest?

Also look again at Ruth 1:9. What did Naomi suggest at that time?

3. What were the details of Naomi's plan, according to verse 3? (Please note—this is very specific advice. Make a list of the aspects of Naomi's instruction.)

And what were the continued details of Naomi's plan, according to verse 4? (Keep your list going!)

Upon Ruth's completion of all Naomi's instructions, who would then have the final say in the matter (verse 4)?

4. What did Ruth reply to Naomi after she had unveiled her plan (verse 5)?

5. And how did Ruth respond to Naomi's instructions (verse 6)?

...and Your Heart's Response

• What character qualities do you observe here in...

   ...Naomi?

   ...Ruth?

• As I combed through this scene from the book of Ruth and took into consideration the fact that Ruth followed Naomi's advice to the letter, four marks of a trusted friend seemed evident.

Mark #1—A trusted friend is caring—Naomi sought "rest" for the young widow Ruth. In other words, Naomi did not want Ruth to remain a mere gleaner in the fields of others for the rest of her life. Instead, she wanted the best for Ruth. Naomi wanted Ruth to be free from the hard life of a widow—she wanted her to remarry and enjoy the security and stability that a married homelife would provide.

Mark #2—A trusted friend is knowledgeable—Naomi knew the customs that governed God's people. And she knew the right way to go about such matters as match-making.

Mark #3—A trusted friend is wise—Naomi gave advice that was intelligent, discreet, and benefitted all parties.

Mark #4—A trusted friend is practical—Naomi left nothing to guesswork but translated her advice into specific steps of action for Ruth.

Now, dear one, take these four obvious marks of a trusted friend from the life of Naomi to heart. Is any one of these marks missing from your life?

And what can you do to cultivate and nurture that missing mark in your character so that you can be a better friend to others? Please be specific.

Cultivating a Life of Character

As the proverb teaches us, it's easy to have *many* acquaintances, but it's hard to be a *true* friend like Naomi was to her Ruth, "a friend who sticks closer than a brother" (Proverbs 18:24)! True friendship is the challenge God sets before us as women after His own heart.

So...how do *you* measure up as a trusted friend? When others think of you, do they think of you as someone they can trust with information? With their problems? For wise counsel? One of the qualities of a godly woman is that she is not a gossip, and another is that she is a teacher of good things (Titus 2:3). A godly woman can be trusted. And a godly woman gives good, godly advice—advice that can be trusted. She is a spiritual instructress.

And if you are married, how do you measure up as a trusted wife? Can your husband trust you? Proverbs 31:11 tells us that the heart of a husband should be able to trust in his wife. Is that true of you? Do you speak well of your husband? Do you, in love, not reveal his faults to others? Do you encourage his pursuits? Do you honor him by the way you live *your* life and by the way you treat him when you are by his side?

And finally, how do you measure up as a trusted mother? Can your children turn to you for advice? Can they trust you to keep the details of their lives private? Have you nurtured a trusting relationship with them? Do you keep your word where they are concerned?

Beloved, think on these things!

Lesson 23

Defining Feminine Excellence

Ruth 3:7-18

Every Christian woman has heard these words many times: "Who can find a virtuous wife, for her worth is far above rubies" (Proverbs 31:10). In fact, as a new Christian, this verse of Scripture was almost the first one I heard when I joined the women's Bible study at my church.

But, dear one, excellence is easier to admire than to define! I have spent the last 28 years attempting (with God's help!) to define and emulate this quality of excellence in my life. In today's lesson you and I are allowed to see the results of one woman's desire to follow God. Ruth, like the Proverbs 31 woman, was "known in the gate." She was noticed by all and admired for her character. Let's see, as we behold Ruth's life, if we can define what it means to be a virtuous woman, a woman of excellence.

God's Message...

1. Read now Ruth 3:7-18. Check here when you are fin-ished. _____

2. Ruth 3:7-13—I hope you remember the details of our last lesson! If not, take a quick look at the previous lesson. When did Ruth approach Boaz (verse 7)?

What announcement did Ruth make to Boaz in verse 9, and what did he reply in verse 12?

After discovering that the woman at his feet was Ruth, how did Boaz respond in verse 10?

…and in verse 11?

The word "excellent" or "virtuous" is used only four times in the Bible to describe women. Note what is said in each case:

Ruth 3:11—

Proverbs 12:4—

Proverbs 31:10—

Proverbs 31:29—

(A professor of the Old Testament shared with me that the most common order in the Hebrew Bible places the book of Ruth right after the book of Proverbs. Imagine! God's description of the Proverbs 31 woman and her many char-acter qualities is followed immediately by the story of Ruth! Truly, one picture is worth a thousand words!)

How did the conversation between Ruth and Boaz end (verse 13)?

3. Ruth 3:14-18—Describe the scene between Ruth and Boaz in the early morning (verses 14-15).

And describe the scene between Ruth and Naomi when Ruth returned home (verses 16-18).

...and Your Heart's Response

• What is Ruth's reputation according to...

...Ruth 2:6—

...Ruth 2:11—

...Ruth 3:11—

What do you think others (your husband, children, neighbors, coworkers, school mates, church friends) say and think about you?

• What character qualities do you observe here in...

...Boaz?

...Ruth? To answer this question about Ruth, look up the scriptures on the next page and jot down the key thoughts or words. Enjoy the journey!

Ruth: The Proverbs 31 Wife [44]

1. Devoted to her family
   Ruth 1:15-18   Proverbs 31:10-12,23

2. Delighting in her work
   Ruth 2:2   Proverbs 31:13

3. Diligent in her labor
   Ruth 2:7,17,23   Proverbs 31:14-21,24,27

4. Dedicated to godly speech
   Ruth 2:10,13   Proverbs 31:26

5. Dependent on God
   Ruth 2:12   Proverbs 31:25b,30

6. Dressed with care
   Ruth 3:3   Proverbs 31:22,25a

7. Discreet with men
   Ruth 3:6-13   Proverbs 31:11-12,23

8. Delivering blessings
   Ruth 4:14-15   Proverbs 31:28-29,31

Cultivating a Life of Character

Dear one, the many sterling character qualities embodied in Ruth's example comprise God's lifetime goal for both you and me as women after His own heart! Whether you are married or not, godly character is always the goal—and the prize—we are to pursue.

And Ruth's life of character developed at a cost! It was the product of a journey that began with a difficult decision—to leave her home, her family, her nation, and her gods. Yet this dear woman of excellence chose to leave the known for the unknown—a decision that proved to be life-changing. The cultivation of a life of character began on that day.

Now here's your exercise in character building:

1. Write today's date here _____

2. Commit yourself to work for the next three months on establishing and/or bettering three character qualities that you admire in Ruth.

   —

   —

   —

3. Choose a friend to be accountable to and set up a time to talk about your character-building exercise three months from today, which will be on _____.

4. Commit yourself through prayer to a lifetime of cultivating character! May it be said of you, "Everyone knows that you are a woman of excellence!"

Lesson 24

Defining Masculine Excellence

Ruth 4:1-12

s I'm busy writing this book, my husband, Jim, is working away on his children's book for our grandson Jacob, *God's Wisdom for Little Boys*. This is a fun, rhyming poem that walks through a roll call of virtues and godly traits for little boys.

Well, in Boaz we see a "big boy" who was described in Ruth 2:1 as "a man of great wealth," meaning a man of valor. Boaz is a fitting complement to our Ruth, who defined *feminine* excellence for us. Let's look now to Boaz for a definition of *masculine* excellence!

God's Message...

1. Read now Ruth 4:1-12. Check here when you are finished. _____

2. Look again at Ruth 3:9. The following definition and description of the responsibilities of a "kinsman" or "close relative" should help you to understand this scene and what Boaz did next.

"The Hebrew word *goel* meaning next of kin has a technical meaning in Hebrew law. The next of kin had certain duties and privileges, among them being that of redeeming the land or person of a kinsman who had been compelled to sell his land or himself through poverty. To draw a portion of a kinsman's mantle over one's self was the legal way of claiming protection and redemption. A kinsman redeemer must be able and willing to redeem and pay the redemption price in full."[45]

3. Ruth 4:1-6—Briefly describe this official meeting and legal negotiations involving the kinsman who was closest in lineage to Naomi and Ruth.

In the end, why did this kinsman decline his responsibility (verse 6)?

4. Ruth 4:7-10—Now briefly describe this public legal transaction that relieved the near kinsman of his duty and passed the role of kinsman redeemer on to Boaz.

What ramifications did this ceremony have on…

…Naomi (verse 9)—

...Ruth (verse 10)—

...Boaz (verses 9-10)—

5. Ruth 4:11-12—What are the blessings the elders and the people prayed for concerning Boaz's marriage to Ruth?

...and Your Heart's Response

- How well do you do at sitting still when major issues whirl about your life? Do you patiently allow God to work through others, or do you try your hand at manipulation or wring your hands in bothered worry? Did you notice that Ruth and Naomi are not present in this passage? Yet their very absence and silence speaks volumes about yet another character quality. They were willing to patiently "sit still" (Ruth 3:18) and trust God to work through others. How can you be more like these two holy women of old who trusted in God and were not "afraid with any terror" (1 Peter 3:5-6)?

- I am so very grateful to my dear husband, Jim (my own excellent husband!), for the following notes from his teaching material on the man Boaz and the many outstanding character qualities that marked his life. I am delighted to share them with you here.

Boaz: A Virtuous Man

• Diligent—Boaz is described as "a man of great wealth" (Ruth 2:1), and we see him carefully and thoughtfully overseeing his property.

• Friendly—Boaz greeted his workers with warmth, and even welcomed the stranger named Ruth (2:4,8).

• Merciful—Noticing Ruth at work, Boaz asked about her situation and acted on her behalf (2:7).

• Godly—Boaz asked Jehovah to bless Ruth in return for her care for Naomi (2:12).

• Encouraging—Boaz pointed out Ruth's strong qualities and spoke of them to cheer her on (2:12; 3:11).

• Generous—Although Ruth needed food and was willing to work for it, Boaz gave her extra (2:15).

• Kind—When Ruth reported the considerate ways of Boaz, Naomi thanked God for His kindness shown to both of them through Boaz (2:20).

• Discreet—Boaz exhibited wise discretion by sending Ruth home before daylight (3:14).

• Faithful—Following through on his promise to Ruth, Boaz "went to court" to clear the way to marry her (4:1).[46]

Cultivating a Life of Character

Here we are, two women after God's own heart, studying the Bible together...and God uses the portrait of a *man* of character, Boaz, to teach us about godly excellence. Oh, dear sister, I think there is much here for us to take to heart!

1. Are you single? Then look for these qualities in the man you may seek to marry. Don't settle for less than God's best—a virtuous man who is godly, diligent, faithful...(you know the list!).

2. Are you married? Then pray for these character qualities in your husband.

3. And, if you are married, be sure you actively promote these godly traits in your husband by encouraging his efforts to cultivate a life of character.

4. And again, if you are married, actively—and often!—praise your husband when you see these spiritual characteristics exhibited in his life.

5. Are you a mother? Then be sure to instill these qualities in the hearts and minds of your daughters (your young Ruths) and your sons (your young Boazes). Point your children to God's high standards and teach them to embrace His ways as their own. Train each son to be a virtuous man...and each daughter to appreciate men who possess godly virtues.

Lesson 25

Redeeming Love

Ruth 4:13-22

Did you know that only two out of the 66 books forming the Bible are named after women? Ruth is one, and the other is Esther. And both books have inspired all ages through all the ages! It's no wonder the Jews have a particular regard for both books. To this day they read Esther at their Feast of Purim and the scroll of Ruth at their Feast of Pentecost.

In the second lesson of this study, we noted that the books of Judges and Ruth give us an unvarnished description of the history of God's people over a period of roughly three centuries. Judges teaches us that turning away from Jehovah incurs severe punishment and that turning back to God restores joy and well-being. And Ruth, our beautiful little book of Ruth, points to our loving Lord's redeeming work in the lives of three people who remained strong in character and faithful to Him while the society around them was collapsing in moral decay.

Today, dear one, we witness firsthand God's redeeming love and His redeeming work in the lives of Ruth, Naomi, and Boaz...the same redemption God extends to you and me today.

God's Message...

1. Read now Ruth 4:13-22. Check here when you are finished. _____

2. Ruth 4:13-16—Note here the wondrous events of verse 13 and God's part in these events.

   How did the women of the community bless Naomi (verses 14-15)?

   What great blessing did Naomi enjoy in verse 16?

3. Ruth 4:17-22—How did the baby come to be named, and what important lineage did he share (verse 17)?

   Just a note—The name *Obed* means "servant." What a fitting ending for our walk with Boaz, Ruth, and Naomi! God's faithful trio of servants just became four!

   As you read through the genealogy that follows—the genealogy of Jesus Christ!—remember that a handful of the unseen women in the genealogy were humanly unlikely, unworthy, and unfit...except for God's redeeming love!

...Tamar, an adulteress, was the mother of Perez,

...Rahab, the harlot, was the mother of Boaz,

...Ruth, the Moabitess, was the mother of Obed, and let's add...

...Bathsheba, an adulteress, was the mother of David's son Solomon.

4. Review of the book of Ruth—As with the book of Judges, enjoy this acrostic that teaches us the high points of the book of Ruth.

Chapter	Acrostic
1	**R** uth returns with Naomi
2	**U** nlimited gleaning from Boaz
3	**T** ime for kinsman redeemer
4	**H** usband redeemer for Ruth[47]

...and Your Heart's Response

• It's wonderful to thrill over the fact of God's abundant outpouring of blessing upon Ruth, Naomi, and Boaz. But, dear one, God is daily pouring out His blessing upon you, too. Take a minute and reflect on His goodness. Make a record here of a few of the "highlights" so that you don't forget. Then give thanks!

• What character qualities do you observe here in...

...Ruth?

Throughout the story of Ruth, we have witnessed her untiring service to her mother-in-law. In the end her service was better than that of "seven sons"! How is your service to your in-laws?

• What character qualities do you observe here in...

  ...Boaz?

From the moment we met Boaz, he has faithfully acted on behalf of others. He didn't rationalize or hesitate. Are there any acts of mercy you need to extend to others? (And don't forget your family members!)

• What character qualities do you observe here in...

  ...Naomi?

Throughout the book of Ruth, Naomi thought only of others. How can you follow her pattern of selfless service?

Cultivating a Life of Character

I hope you're thinking about character! I know I am. There are many "things" you and I can pursue in life. But, dear one, there is *one* "thing" that truly matters—that betters our life and the lives of others. That "thing" is the cultivation of godly character. We've certainly seen the many characters of Judges and Ruth live out the many pursuits referred to in this thought:

> *Fame is a vapor,*
> popularity an accident,
> riches take wings.
> Those who cheer today may curse tomorrow;
> only one thing endures—
> *character.*[48]

May you, dear one, be among the few who choose to pursue the one thing that endures—character!

A Map of the Judges

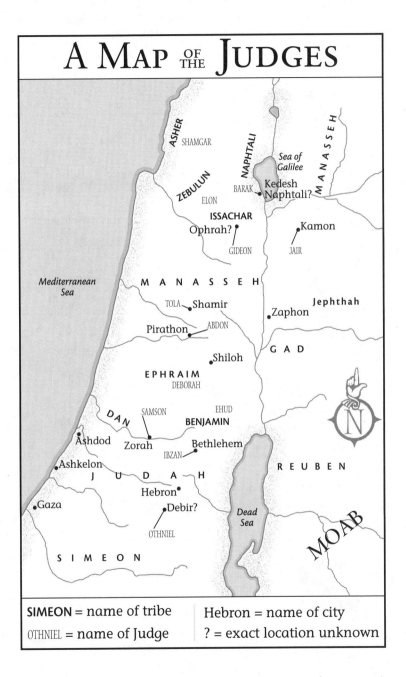

ASHER

SHAMGAR

NAPHTALI

MANASSEH

Sea of Galilee

BARAK · Kedesh Naphtali?

ZEBULUN

ELON

ISSACHAR

Ophrah?

GIDEON

· Kamon

JAIR

Mediterranean Sea

M A N A S S E H

TOLA · Shamir

Jephthah

· Zaphon

Pirathon · ABDON

· Shiloh

G A D

E P H R A I M

DEBORAH

SAMSON   EHUD

BENJAMIN

· Ashdod

Zorah

· Bethlehem

IBZAN

· Ashkelon

J U D A H

R E U B E N

Hebron ·

· Gaza

· Debir?

Dead Sea

MOAB

OTHNIEL

S I M E O N

SIMEON = name of tribe   Hebron = name of city
OTHNIEL = name of Judge   ? = exact location unknown

History of the Judges

Judge	Important Feature	Israel's Oppressor	Time Element	Reference in Judges
1.				
2.				
3.				
4.				
5.				

6.

7.

8.

9.

10.

11.

12.

How to Study the Bible —Some Practical Tips

By Jim George, Th.M.

One of the noblest pursuits a child of God can embark upon is to get to know and understand God better. The best way we can accomplish this is to look carefully at the book He has written, the Bible, which communicates who He is and His plan for mankind. There are a number of ways we can study the Bible, but one of the most effective and simple approaches to reading and understanding God's Word involves three simple steps:

Step 1: Observation—*What does the passage say?*

Step 2: Interpretation—*What does the passage mean?*

Step 3: Application—*What am I going to do about what the passage says and means?*

Observation is the first and most important step in the process. As you read the Bible text, you need to *look* carefully at what is said, and how. Look for:

- *Terms, not words.* Words can have many meanings, but terms are words used in a specific way in a specific context. (For instance, the word *trunk* could apply to a tree, a car, or a storage box. However, when you read, "That tree has a very large trunk," you know exactly what the word means, which makes it a term.)

- *Structure.* If you look at your Bible, you will see that the text has units called *paragraphs* (indented or marked ¶). A paragraph is a complete unit of thought. You can discover the content of the author's message by noting and understanding each paragraph unit.

- *Emphasis.* The amount of space or the number of chapters or verses devoted to a specific topic will reveal the importance of that topic (for example, note the emphasis of Romans 9–11 and Psalm 119).

- *Repetition.* This is another way an author demonstrates that something is important. One reading of 1 Corinthians 13, where the author uses the word "love" nine times in only 13 verses, communicates to us that love is the focal point of these 13 verses.

- *Relationships between ideas.* Pay close attention, for example, to certain relationships that appear in the text:

    —Cause-and-effect: "Well done, good and faithful servant; you were faithful over a few things, I will make you ruler over many things" (Matthew 25:21).
    —Ifs and thens: "If My people who are called by My name will humble themselves, and pray and seek My face, and turn from their wicked ways, then I will hear from heaven and forgive their sin and heal their land" (2 Chronicles 7:14).
    —Questions and answers: "Who is the King of glory? The Lord strong and mighty" (Psalm 24:8).

- *Comparisons and contrasts.* For example, "You have heard that it was said...but I say to you..." (Matthew 5:21).

- *Literary form.* The Bible is literature, and the three main types of literature in the Bible are discourse (the epistles), prose (Old Testament history), and poetry (the Psalms). Considering the type of literature makes a great deal of difference when you read and interpret the Scriptures.

- *Atmosphere.* The author had a particular reason or burden for writing each passage, chapter, and book. Be sure you notice the mood or tone or urgency of the writing.

After you have considered these things, you then are ready to ask the "Wh" questions:

Who?	Who are the people in this passage?
What?	What is happening in this passage?
Where?	Where is this story taking place?
When?	What time (of day, of the year, in history) is it?

Asking these four "Wh" questions can help you notice terms and identify atmosphere. The answers will also enable you to use your imagination to recreate the scene you're reading about.

As you answer the "Wh" questions and imagine the event, you'll probably come up with some questions of your own. Asking those additional questions for understanding will help to build a bridge between observation (the first step) and interpretation (the second step) of the Bible study process.

Interpretation is discovering the meaning of a passage, the author's main thought or idea. Answering the questions that arise during observation will help you in the process of interpretation. Five clues (called "the five C's") can help you determine the author's main point(s):

- *Context.* You can answer 75 percent of your questions about a passage when you read the text. Reading the text involves looking at the near context (the verse immediately before and after) as well as the far context (the paragraph or the chapter that precedes and/or follows the passage you're studying).

- *Cross-references.* Let Scripture interpret Scripture. That is, let other passages in the Bible shed light on the passage you are looking at. At the same time, be careful not to assume that the same word or phrase in two different passages means the same thing.

- *Culture*. The Bible was written long ago, so when we interpret it, we need to understand it from the writers' cultural context.

- *Conclusion*. Having answered your questions for understanding by means of context, cross-reference, and culture, you can make a preliminary statement of the passage's meaning. Remember that if your passage consists of more than one paragraph, the author may be presenting more than one thought or idea.

- *Consultation*. Reading books known as commentaries, which are written by Bible scholars, can help you interpret Scripture.

Application is why we study the Bible. We want our lives to change; we want to be obedient to God and to grow more like Jesus Christ. After we have observed a passage and interpreted or understood it to the best of our ability, we must then apply its truth to our own life.

You'll want to ask the following questions of every passage of Scripture you study:

- How does the truth revealed here affect my relationship with God?
- How does this truth affect my relationship with others?
- How does this truth affect me?
- How does this truth affect my response to the enemy, Satan?

The application step is not completed by simply answering these questions; the key is *putting into practice* what God has taught you in your study. Although at any given moment you cannot be consciously applying *every*thing you're learning in Bible study, you can be consciously applying *some*thing. And when you work on applying a truth to your life, God will bless your efforts by, as noted earlier, conforming you to the image of Jesus Christ.

Helpful Bible Study Resources:

Concordance—Young's or Strong's

Bible dictionary—Unger's or Holman's

Webster's dictionary

The Zondervan Pictorial Encyclopedia of the Bible

Manners and Customs of the Bible,
    James M. Freeman

Books on Bible Study:

The Joy of Discovery, Oletta Wald

Enjoy Your Bible, Irving L. Jensen

How to Read the Bible for All It's Worth, Gordon
    Fee & Douglas Stuart

A Layman's Guide to Interpreting the Bible,
    W. Henrichsen

Living by the Book, Howard G. Hendricks

Leading a Bible Study Discussion Group

What a privilege it is to lead a Bible study! And what joy and excitement await you as you delve into the Word of God and help others to discover its life-changing truths. If God has called you to lead a Bible study group, I know you'll be spending much time in prayer and planning and giving much thought to being an effective leader. I also know that taking the time to read through the following tips will help you to navigate the challenges of leading a Bible study discussion group and enjoying the effort and opportunity.

The Leader's Roles

As a Bible study group leader, you'll find your role changing back and forth from *expert* to *cheerleader* to *lover* to *referee* during the course of a session.

Since you're the leader, group members will look to you to be the *expert* guiding them through the material. So be well prepared. In fact, be over-prepared so that you know the material better than any group member does. Start your study early in the week and let its message simmer all week long. (You might even work several lessons ahead so that you have in mind the big picture and the overall direction of the study.) Be ready to share some additional gems that your group members wouldn't have discovered on their own. That extra insight from your study time—or that comment from a wise Bible teacher or scholar, that clever saying, that keen observation from another believer, and even an appropriate joke—adds an element of fun and keeps Bible study from becoming routine, monotonous, and dry.

Second, be ready to be the group's *cheerleader.* Your energy and enthusiasm for the task at hand can be contagious. It can also stimulate people to get more involved in their personal study as well as in the group discussion.

Third, be the *lover,* the one who shows a genuine concern for the members of the group. You're the one who will establish the atmosphere of the group. If you laugh and have fun, the group members will laugh and have fun. If you hug, they will hug. If you care, they will care. If you share, they will share. If you love, they will love. So pray every day to love the women God has placed in your group. Ask Him to show you how to love them with His love.

Finally, as the leader, you'll need to be the *referee* on occasion. That means making sure everyone has an equal opportunity to speak. That's easier to do when you operate under the assumption that every member of the group has something worthwhile to contribute. So, trusting that the Lord has taught each person during the week, act on that assumption.

Expert, cheerleader, lover, and referee—these four roles of the leader may make the task seem overwhelming. But that's not bad if it keeps you on your knees praying for your group.

A Good Start

Beginning on time, greeting people warmly, and opening in prayer gets the study off to a good start. Know what you want to have happen during your time together and make sure those things get done. That kind of order means comfort for those involved.

Establish a format and let the group members know what that format is. People appreciate being in a Bible study that focuses on the Bible. So keep the discussion on the topic and move the group through the questions. Tangents are often hard to avoid—and even harder to rein in. So be sure to focus on the answers to questions about the specific passage at hand. After all, the purpose of the group is Bible study!

Finally, as someone has accurately observed, "Personal growth is one of the by-products of any effective small group. This growth is achieved when people are recognized and accepted by others. The more friendliness, mutual trust, respect, and warmth exhibited, the more likely that the member will find pleasure in the group, and, too, the more likely she will work hard toward the accomplishment of the group's goals. The effective leader will strive to reinforce desirable traits" (source unknown).

A Dozen Helpful Tips

Here is a list of helpful suggestions for leading a Bible study discussion group:

1. Arrive early, ready to focus fully on others and give of yourself. If you have to do any last-minute preparation, review, re-grouping, or praying, do it in the car. Don't dash in, breathless, harried, late, still tweaking your plans.

2. Check out your meeting place in advance. Do you have everything you need—tables, enough chairs, a blackboard, hymnals if you plan to sing, coffee, etc.?

3. Greet each person warmly by name as she arrives. After all, you've been praying for these women all week long, so let each VIP know that you're glad she's arrived.

4. Use name tags for at least the first two or three weeks.

5. Start on time no matter what—even if only one person is there!

6. Develop a pleasant but firm opening statement. You might say, "This lesson was great! Let's get started so we can enjoy all of it!" or "Let's pray before we begin our lesson."

7. Read the questions, but don't hesitate to reword them on occasion. Rather than reading an entire paragraph of instructions, for instance, you might say, "Question 1 asks us to list some ways that Christ displayed humility. Lisa, please share one way Christ displayed humility."

8. Summarize or paraphrase the answers given. Doing so will keep the discussion focused on the topic; eliminate digressions; help avoid or clear up any misunderstandings of the text; and keep each group member aware of what the others are saying.

9. Keep moving and don't add any of your own questions to the discussion time. It's important to get through the study guide questions. So if a cut-and-dried answer is called for, you don't need to comment with anything other than a "thank you." But when the question asks for an opinion or an application (for instance, "How can this truth help us in our marriages?" or "How do *you* find time for your quiet time?"), let all who want to contribute.

10. Affirm each person who contributes, especially if the contribution was very personal, painful to share, or a quiet person's rare statement. Make everyone who shares a hero by saying something like "Thank you for sharing that insight from your own life" or "We certainly appreciate what God has taught you. Thank you for letting us in on it."

11. Watch your watch, put a clock right in front of you, or consider using a timer. Pace the discussion so that you meet your cut-off time, especially if you want time to pray. Stop at the designated time even if you haven't finished the lesson. Remember that everyone has worked through the study once; you are simply going over it again.

12. End on time. You can only make friends with your group members by ending on time or even a little early! Besides,

members of your group have the next item on their agenda to attend to—picking up children from the nursery, babysitter, or school; heading home to tend to matters there; running errands; getting to bed; or spending some time with their husbands. So let them out *on time!*

Five Common Problems

In any group, you can anticipate certain problems. Here are some common ones that can arise, along with helpful solutions:

1. *The incomplete lesson*—Right from the start, establish the policy that if someone has not done the lesson, it is best for her not to answer the questions. But do try to include her responses to questions that ask for opinions or experiences. Everyone can share some thoughts in reply to a question like, "Reflect on what you know about both athletic and spiritual training and then share what you consider to be the essential elements of training oneself in godliness."

2. *The gossip*—The Bible clearly states that gossiping is wrong, so you don't want to allow it in your group. Set a high and strict standard by saying, "I am not comfortable with this conversation," or "We [not *you*] are gossiping, ladies. Let's move on."

3. *The talkative member*—Here are three scenarios and some possible solutions for each.

   a. The problem talker may be talking because she has done her homework and is excited about something she has to share. She may also know more about the subject than the others and, if you cut her off, the rest of the group may suffer.

Solution: Respond with a comment like: "Sarah, you are making very valuable contributions. Let's see if we can get some reactions from the others," or "I know Sarah can answer this. She's really done her homework. How about some of the rest of you?"

b. The talkative member may be talking because she has *not* done her homework and wants to contribute, but she has no boundaries.

    Solution: Establish at the first meeting that those who have not done the lesson do not contribute except on opinion or application questions. You may need to repeat this guideline at the beginning of each session.

c. The talkative member may want to be heard whether or not she has anything worthwhile to contribute.

    Solution: After subtle reminders, be more direct, saying, "Betty, I know you would like to share your ideas, but let's give others a chance. I'll call on you later."

4. *The quiet member*—Here are two scenarios and possible solutions.

a. The quiet member wants the floor but somehow can't get the chance to share.

    Solution: Clear the path for the quiet member by first watching for clues that she wants to speak (moving to the edge of her seat, looking as if she wants to speak, perhaps even starting to say something) and then saying, "Just a second. I think Chris wants to say something." Then, of course, make her a hero!

b. The quiet member simply doesn't want the floor.

    Solution: "Chris, what answer do you have on question 2?" or "Chris, what do you think about...?" Usually after a shy person has contributed a few times, she will become more confident and more ready to share. Your role is to provide an opportunity where there is *no* risk of a wrong answer. But occasionally a group member will tell you that she would rather not be called on. Honor her request, but from time to time ask her privately if she feels ready to contribute to the group discussions.

In fact, give all your group members the right to pass. During your first meeting, explain that any time a group member does not care to share an answer, she may simply say, "I pass." You'll want to repeat this policy at the beginning of every group session.

5. *The wrong answer*—Never tell a group member that she has given a wrong answer, but at the same time never let a wrong answer go by.

> **SOLUTION:** Either ask if someone else has a different answer or ask additional questions that will cause the right answer to emerge. As the women get closer to the right answer, say, "We're getting warmer! Keep thinking! We're almost there!"

Learning from Experience

Immediately after each Bible study session, evaluate the group discussion time using this checklist. You may also want a member of your group (or an assistant or trainee or outside observer) to evaluate you periodically.

Notes

1. Taken from Elizabeth George, *A Woman After God's Own Heart*® (Eugene, OR: Harvest House Publishers, 1997), pp. 24-29.

2. D. L. Moody, *Notes from My Bible and Thoughts from My Library* (Grand Rapids, MI: Baker Book House, 1979), p. 49.

3. G. Campbell Morgan, *Life Applications from Every Chapter of the Bible* (Grand Rapids, MI: Fleming H. Revell, 1994), p. 70.

4. Sid Buzzell, general editor, *The Leadership Bible* (Grand Rapids, MI: Zondervan Publishing House, 1998), p. 268.

5. John MacArthur, *The MacArthur Study Bible* (Nashville, TN: Word Publishing, 1997), p. 340.

6. Merrill C. Tenney, *The Zondervan Pictorial Encyclopedia of the Bible—Volume 2* (Grand Rapids, MI: Zondervan Publishing House, 1975), p. 259.

7. Moody, *Notes from My Bible*, p. 49.

8. Matthew Henry, *Commentary on the Whole Bible—Volume 2* (Peabody, MA: Hendrickson Publishers, 1996), p. 1078.

9. Albert M. Wells, Jr., *Inspiring Quotations—Contemporary & Classical* (Nashville: Thomas Nelson Publishers, 1988), p. 178.

10. Merrill F. Unger, *Unger's Bible Dictionary* (Chicago: Moody Press, 1980), p. 890.

11. *John MacArthur Bible Studies,* "Church Leadership," 1 Timothy 3:1-13 (Panorama City, CA: Grace to You, 1989), p. 16.

12. Herbert Lockyer, *The Women of the Bible* (Grand Rapids, MI: Zondervan Publishing House, 1975), pp. 40-42.

13. Paul Lee Tan, *Encyclopedia of 7,700 Illustrations,* quoting Jim Elliot (Winona Lake, IN: BMH Books, 1979), p. 271.

14. Moody, *Notes from My Bible*, p. 50.

15. Lockyer, *The Women of the Bible*, p. 42.

16. Ibid.

17. Michael Kendrick and Daryl Lucas, *365 Life Lessons from Bible People* (Wheaton, IL: Tyndale House Publishers, Inc., 1996), p. 76.

18. MacArthur, *The MacArthur Study Bible*, p. 344.

19. *Life Application Bible* (Wheaton, IL: Tyndale House Publishers, Inc., 1988), p. 361.

20. Richard C. Halverson, "The Hero," *Perspective* Newsletter, October 26, 1977.

21. *The Leadership Bible,* p. 279.

22. Arthur Cundall and Leon Morris, *The Tyndale Old Testament Commentaries—Judges and Ruth* (Downers Grove, IL: InterVarsity Press, 1968), p. 122.

23. Florence Littauer, *It Takes So Little to Be Above Average* (Eugene, OR: Harvest House Publishers, 1983).

24. William J. Petersen and Randy Petersen, *The One Year Book of Psalms,* quoting G. Campbell Morgan (Wheaton, IL: Tyndale House Publishers, Inc., 1999), April 22.

25. *Life Application Bible*, p. 371.

26. Eleanor Doan, *The Speaker's Sourcebook*, quoting Oren Arnold (Grand Rapids, MI: Zondervan Publishing House, 1977), p. 46.

27. MacArthur, *The MacArthur Study Bible,* p. 353.

28. Charles R. Swindoll, *The Tale of the Tardy Oxcart* (Nashville: Word Publishing, 1998), pp. 181-82.

29. Wells, *Inspiring Quotations,* quoting J. B. Chapman, p. 22.

30. Cundall and Morris, *Judges and Ruth,* pp. 154-55.

31. Doan, *The Speaker's Sourcebook,* quoting William Ellery Channing, p. 47.

32. Kendrick and Lucas, *365 Life Lessons*, p. 82.

33. Ibid., p. 83.

34. Moody, *Notes from My Bible,* p. 50.

35. Curtis Vaughn, *The New Testament from 26 Translations,* quoting *The New Testament According to the Eastern Texts* by George M. Lamsa (Grand Rapids, MI: Zondervan Publishing House, 1967), p. 1017.

36. Barry Huddleston, *The Acrostic Bible* (Portland, OR: Walk Thru the Bible Press, Inc., 1978).

37. Herbert Lockyer, *All the Books and Chapters of the Bible* (Grand Rapids, MI: Zondervan Publishing House, 1978), p. 67.

38. *The Leadership Bible*, p. 301.

39. Lockyer, *All the Books and Chapters of the Bible,* p. 68.

40. Morgan, *Life Applications,* p. 77.

41. Both quotes from MacArthur, *The MacArthur Study Bible,* p. 366.

42. Morgan, *Life Applications*, p. 77.

43. Frank S. Mead, *12,000 Religious Quotations,* quoting Ralph Waldo Emerson with the pronoun gender changed (Grand Rapids, MI: Baker Book House, 1989), p. 155.

44. MacArthur, *The MacArthur Study Bible,* p. 373.

45. Alan M. Stibbs, general editor, *Search the Scriptures* (Downers Grove, IL: InterVarsity Press, 1979), p. 208.

46. Elizabeth George, *Women Who Loved God—365 Days with the Women of the Bible* (Eugene, OR: Harvest House Publishers, 1999), May 28.

47. Huddleston, *The Acrostic Bible.*

48. Horace Greeley.

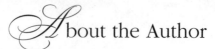 bout the Author

Elizabeth George is a bestselling author and speaker whose passion is to teach the Bible in a way that changes women's lives. For information about Elizabeth's books or speaking ministry, to sign up for her mailings, or to share how God has used this book in your life, please write to Elizabeth at:

Elizabeth George
P.O. Box 2879
Belfair, WA 98528

Toll-free phone/fax: 1-800-542-4611
www.elizabethgeorge.com

Books by Elizabeth George

A Woman After God's Own Heart® Series

A Woman After God's Own Heart®
A Woman After God's Own Heart™ Audiobook
A Woman After God's Own Heart® Deluxe Edition
A Woman After God's Own Heart® Growth & Study Guide
A Woman After God's Own Heart® Prayer Journal

A Woman After God's Own Heart® Bible Study Series

Becoming a Woman of Beauty & Strength—Esther
Experiencing God's Peace—Philippians
Growing in Wisdom & Faith—James
Pursuing Godliness—1 Timothy
Putting on a Gentle & Quiet Spirit—1 Peter
Walking in God's Promises—Sarah

Other books by Elizabeth George

Beautiful in God's Eyes
God Lights My Path
God's Wisdom for Little Girls—Virtues and Fun in Proverbs 31
The Lord Is My Shepherd
Loving God with All Your Mind
A Woman's High Calling
A Woman's High Calling Growth & Study Guide
A Woman's Walk with God
A Woman's Walk with God Growth & Study Guide
Women Who Loved God—365 Days with the Women of the Bible